STUDY NOTES

CURRENT AFFAIRS April 2023

CONTENT TABLE

CURRENT AFFAIRS APRIL 2023

APRIL 2023

CURRENT AFFAIRS

Bajaj Allianz General Insurance & actyv.ai Partners to Offer Insurance Products

Bajaj Finserv's insurance subsidiary, Bajaj Allianz General Insurance Company has entered into a partnership with actyv.ai, the Singapore-headquartered enterprise under the Insurance Regulatory and Development Authority of India (IRDAI), to offer insurance products to MSME (Ministry of Micro, Small & Medium enterprises) through their technology platform and the partner ecosystem across the Supply chain.

Bajaj Allianz General Insurance, a private general insurer, will leverage the technology stack of the actyv.ai platform by offering innovative insurance products to champion the sustainability of suppliers, distributors and retailers. With this collaboration, Bajaj Allianz will offer bite-sized commercial insurance products like fire and burglary, in addition to group health products like personal accident, hospital cash, credit-linked health plans and group health plans.

About Bajaj Allianz General Insurance

- Headquarters : Pune, Maharashtra
- Managing director (MD) and chief executive director (CEO) : Tapan Singhel
- Bajaj Allianz General Insurance Company Limited is a joint venture (JV) between Bajaj Finserv Limited (recently demerged from Bajaj Auto Limited) and Allianz SE.

About actyv.ai

- Founded : 2019
- Founder and Global CEO of actyv.ai : Raghu Subramanian

SEBI proposals clear the air on ESG investments

Capital Market Regulator Securities and Exchange Board of India (SEBI) came out with a holistic regulatory framework for ESG disclosures by India Inc, investors, and rating agencies to facilitate a balanced approach to ESG. In order to enhance the reliability of ESG disclosures, the BRSR (Business Responsibility and Sustainability Report) Core should be introduced, which contains a limited set of key performance indicators (KPIs).

Quantifiable parameters

According to SEBI, initially top 150 listed companies will have to disclose and obtain a reasonable assurance on BRSR Core parameters from FY24 and that will be gradually extended to the top 1,000 listed entities by FY27. The parameters are quantifiable under 9 broad themes - such as change in GHG footprint, change in water footprint, investing in reducing its environmental footprint, embracing circularity (details related to waste management by the entity), enhancing employee well-being and safety, enabling gender diversity in business, enabling inclusive development, and fairness in engaging with customers and suppliers.

Under these themes, there are about 50 KPIs to facilitate comparability of the disclosures. The BRSR core contains factors that are relevant to both the manufacturing and service sectors and are more relevant especially in the Indian context, as attributes such as job creation and inclusive development are considered. To start with, SEBI stated that these requirements of disclosure and assurance should be applicable to the top 250 listed entities (by market capitalization), on a comply-or-explain basis from FY25 and FY26, respectively.

About SEBI

- Established : 12 April 1988 as an executive body and was given statutory powers on 30 January 1992 through the SEBI Act, 1992
- Headquarters : Mumbai, Maharashtra
- Chairman : Madhabi Puri Buch (first woman to lead the SEBI)
- SEBI is the regulatory body for securities and commodity markets in India under the ownership of the Ministry of Finance (MoF), GoI.

Emkay Global gets SEBI's in-principle approval for mutual fund business

Emkay Global Financial Services has received in-principle approval from the capital markets regulator Securities and Exchange Board of India (SEBI) to launch a mutual fund business in India.

About Emkay Global Financial Services

- Founded : 1995
- It offers services such as institutional equity, portfolio management services, wealth management, investment banking and global investing.

Key Highlights

At present, there are 44 MF players with total assets under management of about ₹40 lakh crore with top 10 players accounting for a lion's share of business. Bajaj Finserv was the latest entrant to receive full-fledged mutual fund licence and it has recently filed papers for launching 7 new fund offers. Similarly, billionaire Nitin Kamath-led Zerodha Broking, which has received SEBI's in-principle approval for entering mutual fund business, plans to tie-up with Vasanth Kamath-owned fintech firm smallcase.

MF sponsors subject to having a net-worth of ₹100 crore for contribution towards the net-worth of the Asset Management Company. This net-worth of the AMC has to be maintained till the time it posts profit for 5 consecutive years. Existing players have to maintain a net-worth of ₹50 crore and are required to show net profit in 3 out of the immediately preceding 5 years, including the 5th year.

Nexus Select Trust gets SEBI's approval for REIT IPO

Nexus Select Trust, the retail-focused real estate investment trust sponsored by private equity firm Blackstone, has received the final observations, and go ahead from the Securities and Exchange Board of India (SEBI) for its Real Estate Investment Trust (REIT) initial public offering (IPO) of units. The ₹4,000-crore IPO consists of a fresh issue of ₹1,600 crore while the remaining ₹2,400 crore is through an offer of sale from its main sponsor Blackstone and some other smaller holders.

The REIT aims for a listing by May 15,2023 and is expected to file its final offer document. The REIT's portfolio comprises 17 malls with a total leasable area of 10 million square feet. With an enterprise value of ₹23,000 crore and a debt of ₹3,600 crore, the REIT will still have about $500 million for making acquisitions and adding to its portfolio. It already has an acquisition pipeline of 2.5 msf of assets identified in places such as Ranchi,Jharkhand and Chennai, Tamil Nadu (TN).

IndusInd Bank to enter insurance, mutual funds business & launch digital bank 'Indie'

In a bid to expand its portfolio beyond its core banking business, IndusInd Bank is planning to foray into mutual funds, insurance and broking sectors. The bank is likely to approach the Securities and Exchange Board of India (SEBI), the Insurance

Regulatory and Development Authority of India (IRDAI) and other regulators to get the necessary licences.

IndusInd Bank is also planning to launch its own digital bank 'Indie'. The necessary approvals for all these expansion plans and other logistics by the bank is likely to be completed in about 2 years.

About IndusInd Bank

- Founded : April 1994
- Headquarters : Mumbai, Maharashtra, India
- MD & CEO : Sumant Kathpalia.
- Tagline : We Make You Feel Richer

RBI amends norms on remittances to IFSC under liberalised scheme

The Reserve Bank of India (RBI) has aligned the Liberalised Remittance Scheme (LRS) for International Financial Services Centres (IFSCs) set up under the International Financial Services Centres Authority Act, 2019, with that for other foreign jurisdictions. The resident Individuals may also open a Foreign Currency Account (FCA) in IFSCs, for making the permissible investments under LRS.

Key Highlights

The condition of repatriating any funds lying idle in the account for a period up to 15 days from the date of its receipt is withdrawn with immediate effect. LRS for IFSCs shall now be governed by the provisions of the scheme as contained in the Master Direction on LRS.

What is LRS?

The Liberalised Remittance Scheme (LRS) is part of the Foreign Exchange Management Act (FEMA) 1999 which lays down the guidelines for outward remittance from India. LRS allows Indian residents to freely remit up to USD $250,000 per financial year for current or capital account transactions or a combination of both. Any remittance exceeding this limit requires prior permission from the RBI. Budget 2023 increased tax collection at source (TCS) for foreign remittances under LRS from 5% to 20%. This new rule will come into effect from July 1, 2023.

About RBI

- Established : 1 April 1935
- Headquarters : Mumbai, Maharashtra, India
- Governor : Shaktikanta Das
- Deputy governors : Mahesh Kumar Jain, M. Rajeshwar Rao, Michael Patra and T. Rabi Shankar

NSE revises norms for exclusion from index in case of demerger

The National Stock Exchange (NSE) has come out with new norms to retain the demerged entity of an index constituent in the respective index. A demerged company will remain part of the index, only if the exchange has decided to conduct a Special Pre-Open session (SPOS) for the spun-off entity.

Key Highlights

The change would be applicable to the scheme of arrangement of all companies involving demerger which may be approved by equity shareholders of respective companies on or after April 30, 2023. Additionally, the spun-off business/entity should be included in the index at constant price (which is the difference between the demerged company's closing price one day prior to ex-date of demerger and price derived during SPOS.

However, the spun-off business/entity, which is the newly listed entity, should be removed from the index after 3 days. In case, during the first two days if the spun-off business/entity hits the price band on both days, the exclusion date should be deferred by another three days.

About NSE

- Founded : 1992
- Headquarters : Mumbai, Maharashtra, India
- MD & CEO : Ashishkumar Chauhan

Reliance General becomes first insurer to accept CBDC in partnership with YES Bank

Reliance General Insurance has become the first general insurance company to accept Reserve Bank of India's (RBI's) Central Bank Digital Currency (CBDC) e-Rupee (e₹) for premium payments. The insurer has tied up with YES Bank to facilitate the collection of premiums in digital mode using the bank's e-rupee platform. Customers who have an active e-rupee wallet with any bank can scan Reliance General Insurance's CBDC QR code to make easy, safe, instant, and green payments.

Currently, Reliance General Insurance's physical e-rupee QR code is available at select branches for walk-in customers to scan and pay instantly. Customers who have an active (e₹) wallet with any bank can scan Reliance General Insurance's e₹ QR code to make immediate payment. It plans to make it available at all branches across the country, on its website, and on the Reliance Self-i app in the next few months.

What is e-rupee

e-rupee is a digital token, equivalent to a banknote, and is legal tender or sovereign currency backed by the RBI. It removes all the issues of handling physical cash and offers the same anonymity as a banknote. Moreover, since all transactions are done through an RBI-regulated entity, it reduces banknote-related risks such as anti-money laundering, the counterfeiting of currency, etc.

About Reliance General Insurance

- Founded : 17 August 2000
- Headquarters : Mumbai, Maharashtra
- CEO : Rakesh Jain

About YES Bank

- Founded : 2004
- Headquarters : Mumbai, Maharashtra, India
- MD & CEO : Prashant Kumar
- Tagline : Experience Our Expertise

Business News

UNCTAD: Global goods trade is expected to increase by 1% in the first quarter of 2023

According to the United Nations Conference on Trade and Development (UNCTAD), Global goods trade is expected to increase by 1% in the first quarter of 2023. The trade-in service will grow by 3%. Global trade has reached to more than $32 trillion in 2022 but turned negative in the last quarter. UNCTAD predicted trade stagnation for the first quarter of 2023. As per the report, the uncertainty for trade will remain intact due to ongoing geopolitical tensions, inflation, high commodity prices, etc. UNCTAD said that as most of the trade is done in dollars so a weak dollar would result in increased demand for traded goods. In the fourth quarter of 2022, the global trade for developing countries was impacted.

About UNCTAD

- United Nations Conference on Trade and Development (UNCTAD) is a UN institution that deals with trade and development.
- Founded: 30 December 1964,
- Headquarters: Geneva, Switzerland,
- Head: Secretary-General; Rebeca Grynspan.

EPFO marginally raises interest rate on PF deposits to 8.15% for FY23

EPFO has fixed 8.15% interest rate on employees' provident fund deposits for 2022-23. The decision has been taken by the Employees' Provident Fund Organisation's apex decision making body Central Board of Trustees (CBT). In March 2022, interest rate on EPF deposits for 2021-22 was lowered to four decade low level of 8.1% from 8.5% in 2020-21. This was lowest rate since 1977-78. In 1977-78, EPF interest rate stood at 8%.

About EPFO

EPFO is a statutory body that was established under the Employees' Provident Fund and Miscellaneous Provisions Act, 1952. The organization works under the aegis of the Ministry of Labour and Employment. It helps the central board of trustees in the administration of the Provident Fund Scheme, Pension Scheme and Insurance scheme for the organized sector workers.

Fiscal deficit touches 82.8% of annual target till February

India's fiscal deficit for FY23 touched 14.53 trillion rupees in the 11 months through February - nearly 83% of annual estimates. As per government data the numbers are 17% higher than last year. The country has targeted a budget deficit of 6.4% for the fiscal year ending this month. Data released by the Controller General of Accounts added that the fiscal deficit or gap between the expenditure and revenue collection between April 2022 and February 2023 stood at ₹14.53 lakh crore.

Nokia changes iconic logo for the first time in 60 years

Nokia has changed its iconic logo after nearly 60 years to revamp its brand identity for the first time in the company's history. The new logo is made up of five different shapes making the word NOKIA. Nokia redesigned its logo to avoid being associated with mobile phones, a sector it left almost ten years ago. CEO Lundmark said that Nokia is no longer just a smartphone company, but a "business technology company."

About Nokia

Nokia is a Finnish multinational telecommunication company, established in 1865 in Espoo, Finland. Nokia 1100 was the most popular phone of its time in India w ith a substantial market share before the advent of smartphones. It was known for its durability and sturdiness. 1865 – Nokia is founded as a paper mill in Tampere, Finland. There is currently no logo. 1965 – Nokia begins manufacturing electronics and introduces a simple logo.

India's core sector output rises 6% on year in February 2023

The combined Index of Eight Core Industries (ICI) increased by 6.0 per cent (provisional) in February 2023 as compared to the Index of February 2022. The production of Fertilizers, Coal, Electricity, Cement, Steel, Refinery Products and Natural Gas increased in February 2023 over the corresponding month of last year. The Eight Core Industries comprise 40.27 percent of the weight of items included in the Index of Industrial Production (IIP). The Office of Economic Adviser, Department for Promotion of Industry and Internal Trade (DPIIT) in the Commerce and Industry Ministry releases the Index of Eight Core Industries.

TDS on interest to be applicable even in death cases if EPF contribution exceeds ₹2.50 lakh

Employees contributing over ₹2.50 lakh to the Employees Provident Fund (EPF) will be liable to pay tax on interest even in case of death. Higher Tax Deducted at Source (TDS) rate will be applicable for employees who have not linked their EPF account with PAN. Higher TDS will also be applicable if employees have invalid PAN. The rules will also apply to General Provident Fund (GPF). However, the threshold will be ₹5 lakh because there is no contribution from employer.

International Finance Corporation to invest Rs 600 crore in Mahindra unit at valuation of up to Rs 6,020 crore

Mahindra & Mahindra said World Bank Group arm IFC will invest Rs 600 crore in a new unit of the company, which is being incorporated to scale up the last-mile electric mobility business. IFC's first investment in an EV manufacturer in the country and the first in electric three-wheelers globally will be in the form of compulsory convertible instruments at a valuation of up to Rs 6,020 crore. The Rs 600 crore investment will result in an ownership of between 9.97 percent to 13.64 percent for IFC in NewCo.

India's e-commerce market is projected to grow from $83 billion in 2022 to $150 billion in 2026

India's e-commerce market is projected to grow from $83 billion in 2022 to $150 billion in 2026, according to FIS 2023 Global Payments Report. The report added that cash use declined from 71 percent of POS transaction value in 2019 to just 27 percent in 2022. The Unified Payments Interface (UPI) has helped e- commerce account-to-account (A2A) payments grow to $12 billion, which is up 53 percent between 2021 and 2022, and digital wallets have also grown from 5 percent to 35 percent of POS value. The Global Payments Report also shows that by 2026 A2A transaction value is expected to grow by 195 per cent to $36 billion.

Govt caps maximum GST cess rate on tobacco products

In order to limit the maximum rate of GST compensation cess on pan masala, cigarettes, the government has made amendments to the Finance Bill. Among other items, GST Compensation Cess has been linked to a ceiling rate of their retail selling price. This rule issued by the government will be implemented from the 1 April 2023. The maximum GST compensation cess rate for pan masala will be 51% of the retail sale price per unit, which is currently levied at 135% ad valorem [according to the estimated value of the goods being taxed].

Women in India own 35% of bank accounts, but only 20% of total deposits

Women own a little over one-third of deposit accounts but only one fifth of the total deposit amount in scheduled commercial banks, a report by the Statistics Ministry showed. It also revealed that only one of four bank employees are women. The report noted that not even one-fourth of the female population holds managerial position across the organisations. Also, their share in unpaid work is much higher than their male counterparts. This comes to around 35.23 percent. Similarly, all the mentioned accounts have over ₹170-lakh crore of deposits, out of which women own around

₹34-lakh crore. The report titled, 'Women and Men in India 2022' showed that the total number of deposit accounts at the end of January 2023 was 225.5 crore, out of which over 79 crore are owned by women.

ArcelorMittal-Nippon Steel India JV signs $5 billion loan deal with Japanese banks

ArcelorMittal SA said its Indian steelmaking joint venture with Asian peer Nippon Steel Corp has entered into a $5 billion loan deal with a consortium of Japanese lenders. The proceeds would be used to fund the expansion of the JV's annual steelmaking capacity at its Hazira plant in India to 15 million tonnes from 9 million tonnes. The JV, called AM/NS India, is owned by AMNS Luxembourg Holding SA, in which ArcelorMittal holds a 60% interest and Nippon Steel the rest. The Japanese banks include Japan Bank for International Cooperation, MUFG Bank, Sumitomo Mitsui Banking Corp, Sumitomo Mitsui Trust Bank, Mizuho Bank, Mizuho Bank Europe NV.

Indian economy to grow 6% in 2023: UNCTAD

United Nations, India's economic growth is projected to decelerate to 6 per cent in 2023 from 6.6 percent in 2022. The UN Trade and Development Conference (UNCTAD) in its latest Trade and Development Report Update released expects global growth in 2023 to drop to 2.1%, compared to the 2.2% projected in September 2022, assuming the financial fallout from higher interest rates is contained to the bank runs and bailouts of the first quarter. The International Monetary Fund (IMF) lowered India's economic growth projection for the current fiscal to 5.9 percent from 6.1 percent earlier.

About UN

- Founded: 24 October 1945,
- Headquarters: New York,
- Secretary general: António Guterres.

Jakson Green partners with NTPC to set up methanol plant

Jakson Green has won a project from state-run NTPC to set up a methanol synthesis facility at its Vindhyachal thermal power plant (TPP) in Madhya Pradesh. The methanol synthesis plant will be a part of NTPC's Vindhyachal TPP with a production capacity of 10 tonnes per day (TPD). Methanol is a cleaner alternative fuel that can be used for various purposes including power generation and transportation. Further, it will help India meet its Paris Climate Change Agreement obligation to reduce carbon emissions by 33-35 per cent by 2030.

WTO revises upwards global trade forecast to 1.7% for 2023

As per fresh estimates made by the WTO Global trade in goods is likely to grow by 1.7 per cent in 2023, following a 2.7 per cent growth in 2022, hit by the effects of the long-drawn war in Ukraine, high inflation, tighter monetary policy and financial market uncertainty. The revised growth projection is, however, better than the 1 per cent growth estimated earlier by the WTO, as the relaxation of Covid-19 restrictions in China has improved expectations. Real global GDP growth at market exchange rates is estimated at 2.4 per cent for 2023 against 2.3 percent predicted earlier. For Indian exporters, who have been fighting a demand slowdown since July last year and may just about manage to slightly exceed FY2022 exports of $422 billion in FY2023, the going is likely to continue to be rough in the new fiscal.

About WTO

- The World Trade Organization is an intergovernmental organization that regulates and facilitates international trade.
- Founded: 1 January 1995,
- Headquarters: Geneva, Switzerland.

Paradip Port handles record annual traffic of 135.36 MMT

Paradip Port has handled a record annual traffic of 135.36 million metric tonnes in 2022-23 against 116.13 million metric tonnes in the last financial year. PL Haranadh, Chairman, Paradip Port Authority has given this information during a press conference in Bhubaneswar. The Pradip port has recorded the highest-ever growth of 19.2 million metric tonnes (16.56 percent) of traffic in a single financial year.

Apple BKC to be the first Apple Store in India

Apple has officially announced its first-ever flagship retail store in Mumbai called 'Apple BKC'. An official teaser has also surfaced on the Apple India Store website. Apple has revealed the banner of its first retail store in India at Jio World Drive Mall, Mumbai, marking the opening of Apple BKC. The store is inspired by the 'Kaali Peeli' taxis art popular in Mumbai. The tech giant plans to open the gates of the store later this month. Apple is expected to open its second store in India in New Delhi at a later date.

Reliance, Jio raise $5 billion in largest syndicated loan in India

Reliance Industries Ltd and its telecom arm Jio Infocomm have raised a total of USD 5 billion in back-to-back foreign currency loans, the largest syndicated loan in India's corporate history. Reliance raised USD 3 billion last week from 55 banks and Reliance Jio Infocomm secured additional credit of USD 2 billion from 18 banks. The USD 3 billion financing closed on March 31 and the add-on facility of USD 2 billion was secured. MLAB refers to Mandated Lead Arranger and Book Runner. Reliance Industries Ltd's (RIL) last syndicated offshore borrowing was a USD 1.45 billion dual-currency financing completed in 2020.

Retail inflation declines to 5.66% in March

Consumer Price Index (CPI)-based retail inflation declined to 5.66 % in March 2023. In February 2023, Consumer Price Index (CPI)-based retail inflation stood at 6.44%.

Cost inflation index number for FY 2023-24 (AY 2024-25) used for LTCG calculation notified by CBDT

Cost Inflation Index (CII) for Financial Year 2023-24 has been kept at 348. This is an increase of 5.14%. CII was kept at 331 for Financial Year 2022-23. The index has been notified by the Central Board of Direct Taxes (CBDT)

Solar Energy Corporation of India gets 'Miniratna Category -I' status

Miniratna Category-I Central Public Sector Enterprise (CPSE) status has been accorded to Solar Energy Corporation of India. SECI is committed to achieving the target of 500 GW of non-fossil fuel-based capacity by 2030. Till date, more than 56 GW project capacities have been awarded to SECI.

Ashok Leyland launches 'Re-AL' electronic marketplace for used commercial vehicles

Truck and bus maker Ashok Leyland has launched its e-marketplace ‘Re-AL’ for used trucks. The e-marketplace seeks to offer customers a range of features to easily find vehicles of their choice, such as verified vehicle images, validated documents as well as evaluation reports.

About Ashok Leyland

- Founder: Raghunandan Saran
- Parent organization: Hinduja Group
- Headquarters: Chennai
- Shenu Agarwal, MD & CEO, Ashok Leyland

Credit guarantee fund scheme for micro and small enterprises

The Credit Guarantee Fund Trust for Micro and Small Enterprises (CGTMSE) has upped the coverage ceiling under its Credit Guarantee Fund Scheme from ₹2 crore to ₹5 crore per borrower for credit facilities extended by lending institutions to Micro and Small Enterprises (MSEs). The changes are effective April 1, when the loan growth to the MSE segment slowed to 13.2 percent year-on-year as on February 24, 2023 against 24 per cent y -o-y as on February 25, 2022. CGTMSE is jointly set up by the Ministry of Micro, Small & Medium Enterprises (MSME), Government of India (GoI) and Small Industries Development Bank of India (SIDBI) to catalyse flow of institutional credit to Micro & Small Enterprises (MSEs).

India's exports up 6% to $447 billion in FY23, imports climb 16.5% to $714 billion

India's imports in Financial Year 2023 (FY23) rose 16.5 per cent to $714 billion as against $613 billion in FY22 while exports saw a rise of 6% to $447 billion in FY23, up from $442 billion in FY22. This was revealed by the data released by the Ministry of Commerce and Industry recently. India's CAD stood at $18.2 billion or 2.2% of GDP in the quarter ended December 2022. India's exports are largely led by petroleum ($94 billion), followed by electronic goods ($23 billion).

WPI inflation eases to 29-month low of 1.34% in March

India's annual Wholesale Price Index (WPI)-based inflation declined to a 29-month low of 1.34 per cent in March 2023 as input prices continued to moderate. This is the 10th straight month of decline in WPI-based inflation. The food index inflation eased to 2.32 percent in March from 2.76 percent in February .

Aadhaar brought down KYC cost to ₹3 from as high as ₹700

Finance Minister Nirmala Sitharaman stated that the cost of KYC has reduced from ₹700 to ₹3 because of Aadhaar. The cost of loan processing has been cut down by almost 75%.

About Aadhar

Aadhaar is a 12-digit unique number issued by the Unique Identification Authority of India (UIDAI). It was launched on 28 January 2009.

Government has raised ₹3,51,000 cr through dated securities in Oct-Dec

According to the quarterly report on debt management for October-December released by the finance ministry government raised ₹3,51,000 crore through dated securities as against the notified amount of ₹3,18,000 crore in the borrowing calendar. Repayments stood at ₹85,377.9 crore. During October- December 2022, the government did not raise any amount through the cash management bills. The net daily average liquidity absorption by RBI under Liquidity Adjustment Facility (LAF) including Marginal Standing Facility and Special Liquidity Facility was at ₹39,604 crore during the quarter.

The average ticket size of loans under PMMY nearly doubled in 8 years

The average ticket size of loans under PMMY has almost doubled as per the State Bank of India's economic research department (ERD). The average ticket size of loans under Pradhan Mantri Mudra Yojana has increased from ₹38,000 in FY16 to ₹72,000 in FY23. The amount of loans disbursed under MUDRA increased from ₹1.33 lakh crore in FY16 to ₹4.50 lakh crore in FY23. The number of loans sanctioned stood at ₹6.23 crore in FY23 against ₹3.48 crore in FY16. The ERD said India's Social Fabric Index (SFI) shows 3.2 times jump from 0.813 in FY17 to 2.640 in FY22. SFI represents the participation of the underprivileged in the formal banking system. The SFI is constructed by SBI using principal component analysis. It includes three variables given below.

India attracts fifth of PE inflows into the Asia-Pacific region

India accounts for one-fifth of private equity inflows into the Asia-Pacific. Private equity (PE) and venture capital (VC) inflows into India reached beyond $61 billion in 2022. India's share of investments in the Asia-Pacific region increased to a fifth from less than 15% a year ago. As per the India Private Equity Report 2023 of Bain & Company, the current year will be a cautious optimism with momentum in sectors driven by domestic consumption and export. PE and VC investment declined 15-30% across most regions. Over 2,000 deals were transacted in 2022. Venture capital and growth equity accounted for almost 90% of deals. $1-billion investments slowed.

Exits slowed to $24 billion from an all-time high of $36 billion in 2021. Traditional sectors dominated the share of exits greater than $100 million. Healthcare and manufacturing showing the largest increase in exit value.

Alibaba splits into six units, plans new IPOs in historic overhaul

Alibaba Group Holding Ltd. plans to split its $220 billion empire into six units that will individually raise funds and explore initial public offerings , the biggest overhaul of China's online commerce leader since its inception more than two decades ago. The move frees up the Chinese company's main divisions from e-commerce and media to the cloud to operate with far more autonomy, laying the foundation for future spinoffs and market debuts. Alibaba's announcement coincided with the return of its billionaire co-founder Jack Ma to China after more than a year abroad. Alibaba is ready to tap investors and public markets after the Xi Jinping administration's clampdown on internet spheres wiped out more than $500 billion of its value. Alibaba has had previous success with spinoffs. It hived off Alipay in 2010, an unpopular move that led to Ant Group Co's creation.

IOCL to invest ₹61,077-cr to set up petrochemical complex at Paradip

State-run Indian Oil Corporation (IOCL) have approved setting up a petrochemical complex at Paradip in Odisha at an estimated cost of ₹61,077 crore. The project will be the oil marketing company's (OMC) largest-ever investment at a single location.

About IOCL

- IOCL Chairman Shrikant Madhav Vaidya,
- Founded: 30 June 1959,
- Headquarters: New Delhi.

NSE Comes Up With New Migration Policy For SMEs To Shift To Main Board

The National Stock Exchange of India (NSE) has revised the eligibility criteria for SMEs looking to switch from its SME platform to the main board. The new guidelines require SMEs to list on the SME platform for at least three years along with a minimum net worth of Rs 50 crore and at least 1,000 public shareholders on the last day of the preceding quarter from the date of application before moving to the main board. Effective from April 20, the applicant company should also have positive cash accruals (earnings before interest, depreciation and tax) from operations for each of the three financial years preceding the migration application.

In addition, the company should have positive PAT (profit after tax) in the immediate financial year of making the migration application to the exchange. Moreover, the paid-up equity capital (amount received by the company from shareholders in exchange for shares of stock) of the applicant should not be less than Rs 10 crores and the market capitalisation shouldn't be less than Rs 25 crores

WayCool launches FMCG subsidiary 'BrandsNext'

WayCool, a Chennai-based food and agri-tech platform announced the launch of a wholly-owned subsidiary 'BrandsNext' to exclusively focus on its fast-moving consumer goods (FMCG) business. Started by Karthik Jayaraman and Sanjay Dasari in 2015, WayCool began as a farm-to-fork agri supply chain platform. In 2018, the company entered the consumer packaged goods (CPG) business with the launch of Madhuram (premium variety rice and pulse brand). It then acquired dairy and ready-to-cook brand Freshey's in 2019. Later, it launched another staples brand 'Kitchenji' to expand its product portfolio. Currently, these three brands together offer 108 SKUs ranging from premium rice varieties, dals and pulses, spices and masalas to idli and dosa batter. The three brands will now come under the BrandsNext umbrella.

Tata Steel Honored With Sustainability Champion Status For 6th Consecutive Time By World Steel Association

Tata Steel has been recognised as 2023 Steel Sustainability Champion by the World Steel Association. The Sustainability Champions were announced today at the worldsteel Special General Meeting of the Board of Members held in Vienna, Austria. Recognised for the sixth consecutive year this year, Tata Steel has been a champion every year since the programme's launch in 2018. This prestigious award acknowledges Tata Steel's efforts to maintain its leadership as a world-class steel producer that is fully committed to the principles of sustainability. The World Steel Association (World Steel) is one of the largest and most dynamic industry associations in the world, with members in every major steel-producing country. World steel represents steel producers, national and regional steel industry associations, and steel research institutes. T.V. Narendran, CEO & Managing Director, Tata Steel.

Toyota launches 'Wheels on Web', company's first-ever online retail sales platform

Toyota Kirloskar Motor (TKM) made an announcement of a new digital platform for customers residing in Bangalore state. This will create smooth and comfortable transactions just by sitting at their homes as they can look, buy and order their preferred vehicle. Named 'Wheels on Web', a Business to Customer (B2C) platform is the first-of-its-kind in the Bangalore region. This is launched to prompt online sales to give an uninterrupted experience.

About Toyota Kirloskar Motor

Toyota Kirloskar Motor Private Limited is an Indian joint venture between Toyota Motor Corporation and Kirloskar Group, for the manufacture and sales of Toyota cars in India. The headquarters are located in Bidadi, Karnataka, near Bengaluru.

Appointment and Resignation

SpiceJet Chairman & Managing Director Mr Ajay Singh takes over as ASSOCHAM President

SpiceJet's chairman & managing director Mr Ajay Singh has assumed charge as the president of Associated Chambers of Commerce and Industry of India (ASSOCHAM). He succeeded Renew Power Managing Director (MD) Mr Sumant Sinha after the completion of his tenure as Chairman of ASSOCHAM on Mar 28, 2023.

About ASSOCHAM

- Founded : 1920
- Headquarters : New Delhi, Delhi, India
- The ASSOCHAM is a non-governmental trade association and advocacy group

Prof Dr Renu Cheema Vig appointed as Vice Chancellor of Punjab University

The Vice-President, Shri Jagdeep Dhankhar, who is also the Chancellor of Punjab University appointed Prof. (Dr.) Renu Cheema Vig, as the Vice Chancellor of Punjab University. Exercising the powers conferred by Section 10 of the Punjab University Act 1947, Shri Dhankhar made the appointment of Prof. Vig for a term of 3 years. Consequently, a three member search-cum-selection committee was constituted on March 21, 2023, for recommending names for the position.

Bollywood actor Ranveer Singh named Star Sports Brand Ambassador

Star Sports, India's Home of Sports, announced Bollywood superstar and sports aficionado Ranveer Singh as its brand ambassador. Ranveer, in his role as 'sutradhaar' for the upcoming season of the "Incredible League", will be involved in creating a stream of immersive and entertaining content which brings alive compelling narratives from the past, present, and future of the league. Star Sports and Ranveer Singh's journey as partners starts with the Opening Weekend of Tata IPL 2023 (March 31,2023 – April 2,2023), continues through the tournament as heroes emerge and stories develop.

UAE president names son Mr Sheikh Khaled as next crown prince of Abu Dhabi

United Arab Emirates (UAE) President Mr Sheikh Mohammed bin Zayed Al Nahyan known by his initials MBZ, has appointed his eldest son Mr Sheikh Khaled bin Mohamed as crown prince of Abu Dhabi, the oilrich capital of the Gulf state. Mr Sheikh Khaled bin Mohamed bin Zayed Al Nahyan is a member of the Abu Dhabi Executive Council and Chairman of both the Abu Dhabi Executive Committee and the Abu Dhabi Executive Office.

About UAE

- President : Mohamed bin Zayed Al Nahyan
- Prime Minister : Mohammed bin Rashid Al Maktoum
- Capital : Abu Dhabi
- Currency : UAE dirham

EPFO appoints UTI AMC & SBI Mutual Fund as fund managers

Retirement fund manager Employees' Provident Fund Organisation (EPFO) approved appointment of UTI AMC and SBI Mutual Fund as its fund managers for 3 years. Besides, the EPFO also approved a proposal for early redemption of its investment of around ₹ 700 crore in bonds of troubled Dewan Housing Finance Corporation Ltd (DHFL), at its trustees' meeting held in Hyderabad.

Mr Praveer Sinha reappointed as Tata Power CEO & MD for 4 more years

Tata Power Company Limited (TATA Power) has re-appointed Mr Praveer Sinha as the company's Chief Executive Officer (CEO) and Managing Director for a period of 4 years from May 1, 2023, to April 30, 2027. His present tenure as a CEO and MD is scheduled to conclude on April 30, 2023. Based on the recommendation of the

Nomination and Remuneration Committee, the Board, at its meeting held on March 30, 2023, approved the re-appointment.

About Tata Power

- Founded : 18 September 1919
- Headquarters : Mumbai, Maharashtra, India
- Tata Power Company Limited is an Indian electric utility company & is part of the Tata Group.

HDFC Bank appoints Kaizad Bharucha as Deputy Managing Director & Bhavesh Zaveri as Executive Director

Reserve Bank of India (RBI) has approved the appointment of Kaizad Bharucha as Deputy Managing Director (MD) and Bhavesh Zaveri as Executive Director (ED) of the HDFC Bank for 3 years with effect from April 19, 2023. The RBI approval comes upon the recommendation of the bank's Board of Directors. Prior to his elevation as Deputy MD, Bharucha, who was Executive Director, has been with the Bank since 1995.

About HDFC Bank Limited

- Founded : August 1994
- Headquarters : Mumbai, Maharashtra, India
- MD & CEO : Sashidhar Jagdishan
- Tagline : We Understand Your World

Shreekant M Bhandiwad appointed as chairman of KVGB

Shreekant M Bhandiwad has taken charge as the new Chairman of Karnataka Vikas Grameena Bank (KVGB). He Succeeds Puttaganti Gopi Krishna, who was serving as the chairman of KVGB from 2019 to 2023. Prior to his joining as Chairman of KVGB, Bhandiwad was heading the Patna circle of Canara Bank, Bihar. P Gopikrishna, repatriated to Canara Bank as Circle Head, Bengaluru, Karnataka.

About Karnataka Vikas Grameena Bank

- Founded : September 12, 2005
- Headquarters : Dharwad, Karnataka, India
- KVGB is an Indian Regional Rural Bank sponsored by Canara Bank.
- It is under the ownership of the Ministry of Finance , Government of India (GoI).

- The bank was constituted after amalgamation of 4 Regional Rural Banks (RRBs) namely Malaprabha Grameena Bank, Bijapur(Vijayapura) Grameena Bank, Varada Grameena Bank and Netravathi Grameena Bank.
- It is a scheduled Bank with share capital contributed in the ratio of 50:15:35 by the Central Government, Government of Karnataka and the Canara Bank respectively.

ANMI elects Vijay Mehta as its 28th National President

The Association of National Exchanges Members of India (ANMI), a pan-India industry body representing market intermediaries and stock brokers, has appointed Vijay Mehta Chairman of Mefcom Capital Markets Ltd, as its 28th President for the year 2023-24. He takes over from the outgoing President Kamlesh Shah, the ANMI. The Association of National Exchanges Members of India (ANMI) is a grouping comprising around 900 stock brokers from across the country.

RBI approves reappointment of N Kamakodi as MD, CEO of City Union Bank for 3 years

The Reserve Bank of India (RBI) has approved the re-appointment of N Kamakodi as Managing Director (MD) and Chief Executive Director (CEO) of private sector bank City Union Bank (CUB). The tenure of his re-appointment would be for a period of three years with effect from May 1, 2023. From May 2011, he was serving the bank as its managing director and chief executive officer. Earlier, the CUB launched a facility for its customers to use Voice Biometric authentication for logging into its mobile banking application.

About CUB

- Established : 1904
- Headquarters : Kumbakonam, Tamil Nadu, India

NASSCOM Appoints Microsoft India's Anant Maheshwari As new Chairperson For 2023 - 24

Information technology (IT) industry body the National Association of Software and Service Companies (NASSCOM) has appointed President & Chief Executive Officer (CEO) of Microsoft India Anant Maheshwari as its chairperson for 2023-24. He takes on the new role from his previous role as Vice Chairperson succeeding Krishnan Ramanujam, President, Business and Technology Services, Tata Consultancy

Services, who served as Chairperson for 2022-23. NASSCOM also announced the appointment of Rajesh Nambiar, Chairman and Managing Director (CMD) of Cognizant India, as its Vice Chairperson for 2023-24.

In addition, NASSCOM also announced its Executive Council for 2023-2025. The new Executive Council will play a strategic role in enabling India's tech sector to lead on the global stage through focused initiatives and programmes. The newly appointed leadership along with President Debjani Ghosh will spearhead the industry to carry out its wide array of objectives to achieve the tech industry's vision of $500 billion by 2030.

About NASSCOM
- Established : 1 March 1988
- The NASSCOM is an Indian non-governmental trade association and advocacy group, focused mainly on the technology industry of India.

Rajesh Kumar Singh takes charge as new DPIIT Secretary

Senior IAS officer Rajesh Kumar Singh assumed the charge of secretary in the Department for Promotion of Industry and Internal Trade (DPIIT). Singh has replaced Anurag Jain, who was appointed as secretary in the Ministry of Road Transport and Highways.

About Rajesh Kumar Singh

Singh is an Indian Administrative Service officer of 1989 Batch from Kerala cadre. He has also held the position of Commissioner of the Delhi Development Authority (DDA). He has also held the position of Secretary of Urban Development and Finance Secretary of the Government of Kerala.

About DPIIT
- The DPIIT is a central government department under the Ministry of Commerce and Industry in India.
- DPIIT was established in 1995.
- It was reconstituted in 2000 with the merger of the Department of Industrial Development.
- Headquarters : New Delhi

Mohammad Shahabuddin takes oath as the 22nd President of Bangladesh

Veteran freedom fighter, jurist and politician Mohammed (Md) Shahabuddin was sworn in as the 22nd President of Bangladesh in Dhaka, Bangladesh for a five-year term. Jatiya Sangsad Speaker Shirin Sharmin Chaudhury administered the oath of office to Shahabuddin. He succeeded Md Abdul Hamid, longest serving president in the history of Bangladesh for two consecutive terms.

About Mohammed (Md) Shahabuddin

Shahabuddin was a leader of the Awami League's student and youth wings and took part in the 1971 Liberation War. He was imprisoned following the 1975 assassination of Sheikh Mujibur Rahman, the father of Prime Minister Hasina. In 1982, he was inducted into the country's judicial service. During his career, he served as District and Sessions Judge and Anti Corruption Commissioner (ACC) Commissioner.

About Bangladesh

- Prime Minister : Sheikh Hasina
- Capital : Dhaka
- Currency : Taka

Center appoints Arun Sinha as National Technical Research Organisation chairman

The Government has appointed Arun Sinha as Chairman of the National Technical Research Organisation (NTRO). The post had been lying vacant for over three to four months. Arun Sinha is a 1984 batch Kerala cadre IPS officer. He has served as an advisor of NTRO for two years.

About NTRO

- Formed : 2004
- Headquarters : New Delhi, Delhi, India
- Motto : Aano Bhadra Kritvo Yantu Vishwatah (Meaning - May good thoughts come to me from all four directions)
- It is a technical intelligence Agency under the National Security Advisor in the Prime Minister's Office, India.
- It was formed to strengthen the country's national security apparatus .
- It is under the direct control of the Prime Minister's Office and operates as an autonomous organization.

- The agency follows the same "norms of conduct" as other intelligence agencies in India such as the Intelligence Bureau and the Research and Analysis Wing.

Virat Kohli appointed as brand influencer of HSBC India

HSBC India has appointed former Indian men's cricket team captain Virat Kohli as brand influencer. Kohli will help to amplify HSBC's purpose of 'Opening up a world of opportunity' as it strives to support the ambitions of an aspirational India going global. Additionally, HSBC India is set to launch a multimedia campaign featuring Kohli, aimed at re-establishing the value proposition of banking with the company.

About HSBC India

- Headquarters : Mumbai, Maharashtra, India
- CEO : Hitendra Dave
- The bank has been incorporated in India since 1 January 1983.
- It is a foreign bank under the Banking Regulation Act, 1949 and thus is regulated by the Reserve Bank of India (RBI).

Oliver Dowden sworn in as new United Kingdom's deputy prime minister

The British government named Oliver Dowden as deputy prime minister (PM) replacing Dominic Raab who resigned earlier in the day following a report into claims he bullied colleagues. Dominic Raab's resignation marks the 3rd dramatic Cabinet departure from Rishi Sunak's government even though Sunak has been PM for under 6 months. In the same announcement, lawmaker Alex Chalk was appointed new justice minister, a position which was previously held by Dominic Raab.

About Oliver Dowden

He served in the Boris Johnson government as Minister for the Cabinet Office and Paymaster General from 2019 to 2020 and Secretary of State for Digital, Culture, Media and Sport from 2020 to 2021. In the 2021 cabinet reshuffle, he was moved to the posts of Co-Chairman of the Conservative Party. Currently he serves as cabinet office minister in Rishi Sunak's government.

About UK

- Prime Minister : Rishi Sunak
- Capital : London
- Currency : Pound sterling

Justice Aparesh Kumar Singh appointed as 8th Chief Justice of Tripura High Court

Justice Aparesh Kumar Singh, Judge of the Jharkhand High Court (HC), was sworn in as the 8th Chief Justice (CJ) of the Tripura High Court. Governor Shri Satyadeo Narain Arya administered the oath of office to Justice Singh at a function at the Raj Bhavan. The Supreme Court collegium, headed by Chief Justice D.Y. Chandrachud recommended the name of Justice Singh for the post. The Tripura HC was set up in March, 2013 along with the full-fledged High Courts in Meghalaya and Manipur. All the northeastern states, excluding Sikkim, were earlier under the Gauhati High Court.

Madhav Pai appointed as new CEO of WRI India

The WRI India has appointed Madhav Pai as the new Chief Executive Officer (CEO) of the institute. Pai succeeds former CEO OP Agarwal. In his new role, Pai will lead and oversee WRI India's strategy, operations and activities.

About WRI India

WRI India is an independent policy think tank focussed on developing a low carbon economy.

WRI India's mission

To move human society to live in ways that protect Earth's environment and its capacity to provide for the needs and aspirations of current and future generations. It is legally registered as the India Resources Trust. The India Resources Trust has a licence from WRI to use the trademark "WRI India". WRI India is associated with the Washington DC-based World Resources Institute (WRI), a global research organisation to provide cutting edge analysis to address global environment and development challenges.

About WRI

- Established : 1982
- Headquarters : Washington, D.C. United States
- President & CEO : Ani Dasgupta

Star Sports signs Rishabh Pant as brand ambassador

The Walt Disney Company-owned Star Sports has signed cricketer Rishabh Pant as its latest brand ambassador. The company also has other cricketers as its 'Believe Ambassadors' like Hardik Pandya, Ravindra Jadeja, KL Rahul, and Shreyas Iyer. Star Sports only had two ambassadors in 2017. Cricketer Virat Kohli is also part of this association. The ambassadors will represent different parts of the country as well as different IPL Teams. The 'Believe Ambassadors' represent different parts of the country as well as different IPL Teams.

Rohit Sharma joins JioCinema as brand ambassador for IPL 2023

JioCinema, owned by billionaire Mukesh Ambani's Viacom18, has signed up Rohit Sharma, captain of the men's cricket India, as its brand ambassador. The cricketer will build on the OTT platform's vision of making sports viewing synonymous with digital. In Mar 2023, The Walt Disney Company India-owned channel Star Sports has signed Bollywood actor Ranveer Singh as its brand ambassador.

Indian-origin engineer Mr Amit Kshatriya to head NASA's newly -established 'Moon to Mars' programme

An Indian-origin software and robotics engineer Mr Amit Kshatriya has been appointed as first head of American space agency, National Aeronautics and Space Administration's (NASA's) newly-established Moon to Mars Programme. With this programme, NASA plans to ensure a long-term presence on the Moon to prepare for humanity's next giant leap to the Red Planet. To carry out the agency's human exploration activities on the Moon and Mars for the benefit of humanity. In his new role, Mr Kshatriya will be responsible for programme planning and implementation for human missions to the Moon and Mars.

About NASA

- Founded: 29 July 1958
- Headquarters: Washington, D.C., United States
- NASA Administrator : Bill Nelson
- NASA is an independent agency of the U.S. federal government responsible for the civil space program, aeronautics research, and space research.

Mr Rajib K Mishra takes over as Chairman and Managing Director of PTC India

PTC India Limited, the leading provider of power trading solutions in India, announced that Dr Rajib Kumar Mishra has taken over as the Chairman and Managing Director (CMD) of the company. Dr Rajib Kumar Mishra has worked as Executive Director PTC since October 2011 and was responsible for operations, business development, retail & advisory services. He joined the PTC Board in February 2015 as Director (Marketing and Business Development). He has also served NTPC and POWER GRID in various capacities.

About PTC India Limited

- Founded : 16 April 1999
- Headquarters : New Delhi, India
- PTC India Limited, formerly Power Trading Corporation of India Limited, is an Indian company that provides power trading solutions, cross border power trading, and consultancy services.

Vice Admiral Sanjay Jasjit Singh Assumed Charge As Vice Chief Of The Naval Staff

- Vice-Admiral Mr Sanjay Jasjit Singh became the new Vice-Chief of Naval Staff (VCNS) of the Indian Navy.
- Mr Sanjay Jasjit Singh succeeds Mr S N Ghormade, who demitted office on March 31, About Indian Navy:
- Headquarters : New Delhi, Delhi
- Chief of the Naval Staff : Admiral R. Hari Kumar

Reserve Bank of India appoints Mr Neeraj Nigam as New Executive Director

The Reserve Bank of India (RBI) has appointed Mr Neeraj Nigam as the new Executive Director (ED). In his new role, Mr Nigam will be responsible for overseeing several departments including Consumer Education and Protection, Financial Inclusion and Development, Legal, and Secretary. Before his promotion to ED, he served as the head of the Bhopal (Madhya Pradesh) Regional Office for the RBI.

Mr Gianni Infantino re-elected as FIFA president until 2027

Mr Gianni Infantino was re-elected as the president of Fédération internationale de football association (FIFA) until 2027 at the 73rd Congress of the body in the

Rwandan capital Kigali. He has been re-elected as president of FIFA for a 4 year term from 2023 to 2027.

About FIFA

- Founded : 21 May 1904
- Headquarters : Zurich, Switzerland
- The FIFA is the international governing body of association football, beach soccer, and futsal.

Israel's Ex Envoy To India Mr Ron Malka Appointed Chairman Of Adani Group's Haifa Port

The former Ambassador of Israel to India Mr Ron Malka has been appointed as Executive Chairman of Haifa Port Company (HPC), which is owned by a consortium of Adani Ports and Special Economic Zone Ltd (APSEZ) and Israel's Gadot Group. Mr Ron Malka served as the ambassador of Israel to India and non resident ambassador to Sri Lanka and Bhutan, from 2018 to 2021.

About Israel

- President : Isaac Herzog
- Prime Minister : Benjamin Netanyahu
- Capital : Jerusalem
- Currency : New shekel

Sudha Shivakumar appointed as 40th National President of FICCI Ladies Organization (FLO)

Sudha Shivakumar has been appointed as the 40th National President of Federation of Indian Chambers of Commerce and Industry (FICCI) Ladies Organization (FLO), a women-led and women-focused business chamber from South East Asia for the term 2023-24. She succeeds Mr jayanti Dalmia, 39th national president of FICCI FLO (2022-23). As National President, Shivakumar's main focus will be on empowering women by creating an enabling environment that promotes entrepreneurship, industry participation and economic growth of women.

About FLO

- Established : 1983
- Headquarters : New Delhi, India

- FLO was founded as a subsidiary of FICCI, India's premier industry and commerce body.
- FLO at present has 19 chapters across India with about 3,000 business women as its members.

Suzuki Motorcycle India appoints Mr Kenichi Umeda as new Managing Director

Suzuki Motorcycle India Pvt Ltd (SMIPL) announced the appointment of Mr Kenichi Umeda as its new Managing Director (MD). Mr Umeda succeeds Satoshi Uchida, who has completed his term as the MD of the company, SMIPL. Mr Umeda will now be responsible for further growing and strengthening Suzuki Motorcycle India's position in the Indian and overseas markets.

About Suzuki Motorcycle India Pvt Ltd

- Founded: 2006
- Headquarters: Gurgaon, Haryana, India.
- Suzuki Motorcycle India, Private Limited is a wholly owned Indian subsidiary of Suzuki, Japan.
- It was the third Suzuki automotive venture in India, after TVS Suzuki and Maruti Suzuki.

Axis Securities appoints Mr Pranav Haridasan as new MD and CEO

Axis Securities Limited has appointed Mr Pranav Haridasan as its new Managing Director (MD) and Chief Executive Officer (CEO) for a tenure of 3 years. He will succeed the current MD & CEO, Mr B Gopakumar who has been transferred to Axis Asset Management Company as MD & CEO.

About Axis Securities Limited

- Incorporated on : 21 Jul, 2006
- Headquarters : Mumbai, Maharashtra, India
- Axis Securities is a subsidiary of Axis Bank which operates retail broking services through Axis Direct.

Iran appoints UAE ambassador for first time since 2016

Iran had appointed an ambassador to the United Arab Emirates (UAE) for the first time since 2016, amid a realignment of relations between Gulf states and Iran. Iran appointed Reza Ameri as its ambassador to the UAE. He has served as the Director General of the Iranian expatriates' office in the Foreign Ministry.

About Iran

President : Ebrahim Raisi
- Capital : Tehran
- Currency : Iranian rial

Honda Motorcycle & Scooter India appoints Tsutsumu Otani as new President, CEO & MD

One of the leading two-wheeler makers, Honda Motorcycle & Scooter India (HMSI) appointed Tsutsumu Otani as the President, Chief Executive Officer (CEO) and Managing Director (MD). He has succeeded Atsushi Ogata, who headed Honda's Indian two-wheeler operations for three years. Prior to this, Otani was the Vice President at Honda Motor Co. Japan

About HMSI

- Founded : 20 August 1999
- Headquarters : Gurgaon, Haryana, India
- HMSI is the wholly owned Indian subsidiary of Honda Motor Company, Limited, Japan.

Ministry of Corporate Affairs appointed Grant Thornton Bharat to Assist in Capacity Building

The Ministry of Corporate Affairs(MCA) has appointed Grant Thornton Bharat LLP, one of the largest fully integrated Assurance, Tax and Advisory firms in India, to assist in the formulation of an Annual Capacity Building Plan (ACBP) as a part of its efforts to build capacity among its cadre/ posts and other organisations to make them 'future ready' and to meet the requirements of a vision of 'New India'. To enhance the delivery system and create a 'citizen centric, future ready civil service with the right attitude, skills and knowledge aligned to the vision of New India'.

About MCA

- Union Minister : Smt. Nirmala Sitharaman
- Minister of State : Rao Inderjit Singh

MCA extends tenure of IL&FS chairman Chandra Shekhar Rajan till September 2023

The Ministry of Corporate Affairs (MCA) has extended the term of Chandra Shekhar Rajan as non-executive chairman of IL&FS (Infrastructure Leasing & Financial Services Limited) up to September 30, 2023. Besides, the ministry has also extended the term of Nand Kishore as managing director of IL&FS up to March 31, 2024.

About IL & FS

- Founded : 1987
- Headquarters : Mumbai, Maharashtra, India
- IL & FS is an Indian state-funded infrastructure development and finance company. It was an "Reserve Bank of India (RBI) registered Core Investment Company"

Kalikesh Narayan Singh Deo assumed charge as the President of the National Rifle Association of India (NRAI)

He replaced Raninder Singh. Raninder served as the president of NRAI from December 29, 2010 till December 29, 2022 & he completed 12 years of his service. As per the National Sports Code, the Sports Ministry issued a directive that the heads of National Sports Federations (NSFs) cannot hold office for more than 12 years. As per the code, Raninder cannot continue as NRAI chief any further.

About NRAI

- Founded : 1951
- Headquarters : New Delhi, Delhi, India

India was elected to United Nations Statistical Commission for a 4-year term starting in 2024

India has been elected to the United Nations (UN) Statistical Commission for a four-year term starting from 1st January 2024. India received a resounding 46 out of 53 votes, ahead of South Korea (23), China (19), and the United Arab Emirates (UAE) (15). India was elected by secret ballot while Argentina, Sierra Leone, Slovenia, Ukraine, the United Republic of Tanzania and the United States of America were elected by acclamation for a 4-year term of office beginning January 1, 2024.

About UN Statistical Commission

- Established : 1947
- Location : New York, United States
- Chairperson of UN Statistical Commission for the year 2023 : Ms. Gabriella Vukovich (Hungary)

Samantha Ruth Prabhu has been appointed as the brand ambassador of Tommy Hilfiger

Tommy Hilfiger, the premium fashion brand owned by NYSE-listed PVH Corp, has signed Tollywood star heroine Samantha Ruth Prabhu as the new brand ambassador for their women watches category. From now on, Sam will appear in the women's watch ads of the Tommy Hill figure company. As part of the Spring Summer 23 campaign, Samantha will appear in the advertisements of the Tommy Hill figure release in the month of April, 2023. Tommy company is a global brand. This company offers products for every person to have their own personal style and design.

Suzlon board appoints J P Chalasani as new Chief Executive Officer

The board of members of Wind and turbine manufacturer Suzlon Energy has appointed J P Chalasani as the new Chief Executive Officer (CEO) of the company. He has replaced Ashwani Kumar, who resigned from the post on account of personal reasons. He joined Reliance Group (undivided) as a Vice President in 1995. He also served as the first CEO and the Director on the Board of BSES Rajdhani and BSES Yamuna Power Limited. He had been Group CEO of Suzlon from April 2016 to July 2020. He continued as Strategic Advisor to the Suzlon Group thereafter. He was also the Group CEO and Managing Director of Punj Lloyd.

About Suzlon Energy Limited

- Founded : 1995
- Headquarters : Pune, Maharashtra, India
- Suzlon Energy Limited is an Indian multinational wind turbine manufacturer.

K Krithivasan appointed as CEO of Tata Consultancy Services

Tata Consultancy Services (TCS) has appointed K Krithivasan as its new Chief Executive Officer (CEO) and Managing Director (MD) of the company. He will take over the post with effect from June 01, 2023 for a tenure of 5 years which ends in Feb 2027. He will replace outgoing CEO Rajesh Gopinathan, who was appointed in 2017.

Rajesh Gopinathan, will continue to assist him in a smooth transition till end of September 2023.

About TCS

- Founded : 1968
- Headquarters : Mumbai, Maharashtra, India
- Chairman : Natarajan Chandrasekaran
- TCS is an Indian multinational information technology (IT) services and consulting company.

Justice Apresh Kumar Singh appointed as new Chief Justice of Tripura High Court

In exercise of the powers conferred by clause (1) of Article 217 of the Constitution of India, the President of India appointed Justice Aparesh Kumar Singh, Judge of Jharkhand High Court as the Chief Justice of Tripura High Court. Apresh Kumar replaced Justice T Amarnath Goud, who was serving as the Acting Chief Justice of the Tripura High Court from November 2022. He was appointed as an Additional Judge of the High Court of Jharkhand on 24th January 2012 and confirmed as a permanent Judge on 16th January 2014. He has also served as the Acting Chief Justice of the Jharkhand High Court from the 20th of December, 2022 to the 19th of February, 2023.

About Tripura High Court

The Tripura High Court was established on 23 March 2013 following an amendment to the Constitution of India and the North-Eastern Areas Act of 1971.

ATMA elects Anshuman Singhania as new Chairman and Arnab Banerjee as new Vice-Chairman

Anshuman Singhania, the Managing Director of JK Tyre & Industries Ltd has been elected as the new Chairman of Automotive Tyre Manufacturers' Association (ATMA). Apart from this, Arnab Banerjee, the Managing Director & CEO of CEAT Ltd, has taken over as ViceChairman of ATMA. ATMA was set up in 1975, registered under The Companies Act, as the representative body of the automotive tyre industry in India. ATMA members include Apollo Tyres, Bridgestone India, Ceat, Continental India, Goodyear India, JK Tyre & Industries, MRF and TVS Tyres. 8 large tyre companies comprising a mix of Indian and International tyre majors and representing over 90% of production of tyres in India are members of the Association.

NPCI appoints Vishal Anand Kanvaty as chief technology officer

The National Payments Corporation of India (NPCI) has appointed Vishal Anand Kanvaty as its Chief Technology Officer (CTO). In his new role, Kanvaty will be taking care of the new-age technology and shall be responsible for the transformational journey of NPCI. Kanvaty joined NPCI in 2017. Prior to this he managed the portfolio of Chief Market Innovation as well as Product and Innovations profiles.

About NPCI

- Founded : 2008
- Headquarters : Mumbai, Maharashtra, India
- MD & CEO : Dilip Asbe
- The NPCI is an umbrella organization for operating retail payments and settlement systems in India.
- It is an initiative of the Reserve Bank of India (RBI) and Indian Banks' Association (IBA) under the provisions of the Payment and Settlement Systems Act, 2007, for creating a robust Payment & Settlement Infrastructure in India.

RBI approves re-appointment of Sanjay Agarwal as MD & CEO of AU Small Finance Bank

The Reserve Bank of India (RBI) has approved the re-appointment of Sanjay Agarwal as Managing Director (MD)& Chief Executive Officer (CEO) of Jaipur headquartered AU Small Finance Bank for 3 years with effect from 19 April 2023 till April 18, 2026. The central bank also approved the re-appointment of Uttam Tibrewal as Whole Time Director for 3 years with effect from 19 April, 2023.

About AU Small Finance Bank Limited

- Founded : 1996 (Converted to a small finance bank on 19 April 2017)
- Headquarters : Jaipur, Rajasthan, India
- Tagline : Chalo Aage Badhe

Karnataka Bank appoints Sekhar Rao as interim CEO

The Reserve Bank of India (RBI) has approved the appointment of Sekhar Rao as interim managing director (MD) and chief executive officer (CEO) of Karnataka Bank. He has been appointed for a period of three months or till the appointment of regular MD and CEO whichever is earlier. He replaced Mahabaleshwara M S.

About Karnataka Bank

- Founded : 18 February 1924
- Headquarters : Mangalore, Karnataka, India
- Tagline : Your Family Bank Across India

Awards and Honour

Maha Metro receives prestigious 'Asia Book of Record' citation ` Having being awarded Guinness World Records and two Asia Book of Records earlier, Maha Metro Nagpur was honoured with the prestigious Asia Book of Records certification for three different categories. The certification and citation was presented by Deputy Chief Minister of Maharashtra Devendra Fadnavis at Metro Bhawan on March 19. The categories for which Nagpur Metro was presented with Asia Book of Records certification are 'Longest Length of Metro Rail Corridor Construction in Shortest Time', 'First Solar PV System in a Metro Rail Project for Integrated Consumption' and 'Heaviest Single Span Double Decker Steel Bridge Truss over Railway tracks in Urban Area', in Asia.

Nepalese Wicketkeeper-batsman Aasif Sheikh declared winner of 2022 CMJ Spirit of Cricket Award

Nepalese Wicketkeeper-batsman Aasif Sheikh has been declared the winner of the 2022 Christopher Martin-Jenkins Spirit of Cricket Award. The Award is presented every year by the Marylebone Cricket Club (MCC), UK in conjunction with the BBC. The CMJ Spirit of Cricket Award was created in 2013 by MCC and the BBC in memory of former MCC President and BBC Test Match Special commentator Christopher Martin-Jenkins (CMJ), who was passionate about promoting the spirit of the game. He was also awarded the ICC Spirit of Cricket Award for his actions in January of this year.

Aaliya Mir Becomes The First Woman From J&K To Receive Wildlife Conservation Award

J&K's Aaliya Mir gets Wildlife Conservation Award. She is J&K's only female wildlife rescuer. She is best known for her work with snakes. She has rescued Asiatic black bears, Himalayan brown bears, birds, leopards and other mammals. She works as a project manager with Wildlife SOS, a non-governmental organisation. She got the award from LG Manoj Sinha on the International Day of Forests (21 March) event.

Assam NGO wins Children's Champion Award 2023

Students' Welfare Mission, popularly known as Tapoban, has won the Children's Champion Award 2023. Tapoban is working for special needs and autistic children. The award has been presented by Justice S. Muralidhar, Chief Justice of the Odisha High Court to Kumud Kalita, founder-President of Tapoban. Tapoban, established in 2005, has received award in the health and nutrition category award for its efforts to provide quality care to children with special needs.

Zelensky awarded Poland's highest honour

Volodymyr Zelensky has been awarded Poland's highest Order of the White Eagle award. He has received the award for his service to security, resilience and the defense of human rights. Polish President Andrzej Duda presented the award to Volodymyr Zelensky. The Order of the White Eagle is Poland's oldest and highest decoration.

Indian-American mathematician C R Rao awarded math 'Nobel Prize'

The Indian-American statistician Calyampudi Radhakrishna Rao has been awarded the 2023 International Prize in Statistics , which is statistics' equivalent of the Nobel Prize. It was established in 2016 and is awarded once every two years to an individual or team "for major achievements using statistics to advance science, technology and human welfare. Rao's groundbreaking paper, 'Information and accuracy attainable in the estimation of statistical parameters', was published in 1945 in the Bulletin of the Calcutta Mathematical Society, a journal that is otherwise not well known to the statistics community.

Bharat Biotech wins award at World Vaccine Congress

Bharat Biotech has won the `Best Production /Process Development' award as part of the Vaccine Industry Excellence (ViE) awards at the World Vaccine Congress 2023. The Congress was held during April 3-6 in Washington, USA. Hyderabad-based Bharat Biotech was the only Indian company in the list of VIE awards in various categories, including best clinical trial company, best clinical trial network, best central/speciality laboratory award, best contract research organisation, best production/process development award, among others. Bharat Biotech is the world's first producer of intranasal Covid -19 vaccine, iNcovacc. Its intramuscular vaccine, Covaxin, is part of India's public vaccination programme and was also exported.

Kumar Mangalam Birla received AIMA's 'Business Leader of the Decade' award

Kumar Mangalam Birla, chairman of Aditya Birla Group, won the prestigious 'Business Leader of the Decade' award at All India Management Association's (AIMA) 13th Managing India Awards ceremony. The annual event to facilitate the titans of the industry, held in New Delhi. Tata Steel Chairman T V Narendran was facilitated with the 'AIMA-JRD Tata Corporate Leadership' award.

Amit Shah to confer Maharashtra Bhushan Award to social activist Appasaheb Dharmadhikari

Renowned social worker and reformer Dattatreya Narayan Dharmadhikari alias Appasaheb Dharmadhikari will be honored with the Maharashtra Bhushan Award by Union Home Minister Amit Shah. Appasaheb Dharmadhikari was nominated for the prestigious 2022 Maharashtra Bhushan Award. It is the highest civilian award conferred by the government of Maharashtra.

Utsa Patnaik wins Malcolm Adiseshiah Award 2023

Utsa Patnaik has been chosen for the Malcolm Adiseshiah Award 2023. Utsa Patnaik is a renowned economist of national and international repute.

Indian-American CEO Raj Subramaniam presented with Pravasi Bharatiya Samman

Raj Subramaniam, the Indian-American CEO of global transportation giant FedEx , has been presented with the prestigious Pravasi Bharatiya Samman, the highest civilian award given by India to persons of Indian origin and Indian diaspora.

Ranking and Indexes

Mukesh Ambani is the only Indian in Hurun Global Rich list's top 10

According to the Hurun Global Rich List released Reliance Industries (RIL) Chairman and Asia's richest man Mukesh Ambani became the only Indian to feature in the list of top 10 billionaires across the world. Despite a 20 per cent dip in wealth, the RIL boss occupied ninth rank globally with a net worth of $82 billion. The billionaire has also retained the wealthiest Asian title for the third consecutive year. Ambani ranked first, followed by Gautam Adani with a net worth of $53 billion among Indian billionaires. The richest new entrant from India, Rekha Rakesh Jhunjhunwala & family, tops the list of top 16 new Indian entrants in 2023 M3M Hurun Global Rich List.

Agriculture sector employs highest female workers

According to the annual Periodic Labour Force Survey (PLFS) Report 2021-22, agriculture sector has the highest estimated percentage distribution of female workers followed by manufacturing. Nearly 63% workers are female in the agriculture sector at the pan-India level, while the estimated percentage distribution of female worker in the manufacturing sector is 11.2%. The PLFS report 2021-22 showed that the estimated female labour force participation rate (LFPR) in Haryana on usual status for age 15 years and above is 19.1%. District-wise estimates are not captured in PLFS reports.

26 % of world's population does not have safe drinking water: UNESCO report

26 percent of the world's population does not have safe drinking water and 46 percent lack access to safely managed sanitation, according to a report published by UNESCO at the UN 2023 Water Conference in New York. As per the report, between two and three billion people experience water shortages for at least one month per year, posing severe risks to livelihoods, notably through food security and access to electricity. The global urban population facing water scarcity is projected to double from 930 million in 2016 to 1.7 to 2.4 billion people in 2050. The growing incidence of extreme and prolonged droughts is also stressing ecosystems, with dire consequences for both plant and animal species.

About UNESCO

- Founded: 16 November 1945, London, United Kingdom
- Headquarters: Paris, France
- Head: Audrey Azoulay; (Director-General)

Ladakh, Mayurbhanj Among TIME Magazine's 50 Greatest Places In The World 2023

Mayurbhanj district of Odisha has been listed by TIME Magazine among the 50 extraordinary destinations to explore in its list of the World's Greatest Places of 2023. Apart from Mayurbhanj, Ladakh is the second destination from India to be included in the coveted magazine. The only place on earth to spot the exceedingly rare black tiger is open to visitors again. The Magazine also refers to the other destinations of Odisha including the state capital Bhubaneswar .

Ladakh, Mayurbhanj Among TIME Magazine's 50 Greatest Places In The World 2023

Mayurbhanj district of Odisha has been listed by TIME Magazine among the 50 extraordinary destinations to explore in its list of the World's Greatest Places of 2023. Apart from Mayurbhanj, Ladakh is the second destination from India to be included in the coveted magazine. The only place on earth to spot the exceedingly rare black tiger is open to visitors again. The Magazine also refers to the other destinations of Odisha including the state capital Bhubaneswar.

IIT Delhi enters list of top 50 institutions for engineering in QS Rankings 2023

The Indian Institute of Technology -Delhi has entered the list of top 50 institutions for engineering in the QS World University Rankings by Subject 2023. With a ranking of 48, it is up by seven places from last year. As many as 44 programmes offered by Indian higher education institutions in different disciplines have figured in the top 100 globally. Last year, 35 Indian programmes made it to the top 100. The Delhi University is the Indian varsity with maximum entries (27) followed by Indian Institute of Technology (IIT), Bombay, (25) and IIT-Kharagpur (23). The thirteen edition of the QS World University Rankings by Subject has ranked 66 Indian universities, cumulatively achieving 355 entries, a 18.7 percent increase compared to last year (299).

India falls six spots in Passport Index 2023; UAE ranks number one

Slipping six ranks from last year, the Indian passport has registered the largest global fall in the Passport Index 2023 — ranking at the 144th position this year, with a mobility score of 70. Several nations, like Serbia, have been under pressure to introduce visa requirements for Indian nationals. This year, the United Arab Emirates (UAE) has the highest mobility score of 181, and ranks number one. It was followed by Sweden, Germany, Finland, Luxembourg, Spain, France, Italy, the Netherlands, and Austria, with a joint mobility score of 174.

Elon Musk titled the Most Followed Twitter User

Elon Musk titled as the Most Followed Twitter User. The business tycoon Elon Musk left behind former US President Barack Obama along with Justin Bieber in the number of followers he gained on Twitter. Twitter records that over 450 million people across the world use this famous social networking platform. Out of the total Twitter users, more than 133 million follow this new owner Elon. He acquired this site on October 27, 2023, for worth $44 billion .

India Is Home To The Fifth Highest Number Of Female Billionaires In The World

India is home to the fifth highest number of female billionaires in the world. According to City Index, the United States has the highest number of female billionaires in the world with 92 in total, double that of China in second place with 46. While the US might be home to some of the highest profile male billionaires, 4 out of the 5 richest women in the world, including Walmart heiress Alice Walton, also hail from the states. Germany takes third place with 32 female billionaires , just over a third than that of the US. As the richest woman in the world and Vice Chairman of L'Oréal, French-born Françoise Bettencourt Meyers takes the top spot with a wealth of $81.49 billion. New York-based socialite Julia Koch ($59.65bn) and Walmart inheritor Alice Walton ($60.16bn) are almost tied in third and second places, respectively.

Tripura becomes best performing northeast state in e-procurement, receives award

Tripura became the best-performing state among North Eastern States in implementing e-Procurement. Tripura received this award at a National Workshop on e-Procurement. A National Workshop on e-Procurement was organized by the Ministry of Finance and the Ministry of Electronic and Information Technology. The Tripura government has been recognized for their work in various departments in the last 5 years. The Tripura government has received this award for completing the work within a specified time under the Power Department's Saubhagya Yojana. Tripura also gets the title of the best performer in agriculture, and panchayat self-employment.

Mumbai among 19 cities with the best public transport in the world, and it's the only one from India

Mumbai, Maharashtra's capital has featured in the list of top twenty cities with best public transport in the world. The city's Suburban Railways, which was the first passenger railway to be built by the British East India Company, forms the backbone of public transport for a population of 12.5 million. The list that has been released by Time Out, the publisher of global city guides. Maharashtra's capital city Mumbai featured in the nineteenth rank on the list.

The world's best cities for public transit –

- Berlin, Germany,
- Prague, Czech Republic,
- Tokyo, Japan,
- Copenhagen, Denmark,
- Stockholm, Sweden.

MRF emerges as 'second strongest tyre brand in the world'

MRF Limited has emerged as the second strongest tyre brand in the world according to the latest report by Brand Finance on the Most Valuable and Strongest Tyre Brands in the world. MRF has scored 83.2 out of 100 in brand strength and was awarded a AAA- brand rating. French company Michelin has been rated both the most valuable and strongest tyre brand. There are two Indian tyre companies in the Top 15 list of most valuable – MRF Tyres and Apollo Tyres. MRF Tyres, ranked 13th, sees its brand value grow 3% to $0.3 billion and has seen a sizeable jump of 15 ranks in the latest industry ranking list. At No. 15 is Apollo Tyres with a brand value of $0.6 billion.

Andhra Pradesh's Jagan Mohan Reddy most wealthiest CM in India

Twenty-nine of the 30 incumbent Chief Ministers are crorepatis with Andhra Pradesh's Jagan Mohan Reddy having the highest assets totalling ₹510 crore, according to poll affidavits analysed by the Association for Democratic Reforms (ADR). West Bengal Chief Minister Mamata Banerjee has the lowest total assets of about ₹15 lakh, the ADR said. Non-bailable offences with over five years of imprisonment, the report said. The top three Chief Ministers in terms of assets are Andhra Pradesh's Jagan Mohan Reddy (over ₹510 crores), Arunachal Pradesh's Pema Khandu (over ₹163 crores), and Odisha's Naveen Patnaik (over ₹63 crores), according to the ADR. The three CMs with the lowest declared assets are — West Bengal's Mamata Banerjee (over ₹15 lahks), Kerala's Pinarayi Vijayan (over ₹1 crore) and Haryana's Manohar Lal (over ₹1 crore).

Mumbai ranks among the world's tree-rich cities in 2022, the second time in a row

India's commercial capital Mumbai has been included in the World Tree City 2022 list, for the second consecutive year. The Arbor Day Foundation Chief Executive Dan Lambe has awarded the TCW certificate signed by Hiroto Mitsugi to the BMC authorities. The United Nations Food & Agriculture Organisation (FAO) and ADF conduct the TCW programme and in the past 50 years, the ADF has planted more than 35 crore trees worldwide, with a target of 50 crore more trees by 2027.

Shah Rukh Khan tops TIME 100 Reader Poll, defeats Lionel Messi, Prince Harry

Shah Rukh Khan the man that gave Bollywood its biggest hit "Pathaan' since the industry seemed to have been suffering in box office collections in the post-covid era, has now ranked highest in TIME 100 Reader Poll. Shah Rukh Khan, 57, topped the list of most influential people around the world, for TIME magazine's 100th edition of the list. Shah Rukh Khan received 4 percent of the 1.2 million votes cast by readers in the 2023 TIME100 poll. In second place are the Iranian women who are protesting for their rights. They garnered 3% of the votes. The woman also won the magazine's 2022 Person of the Year reader poll. In third place, with 2% of the votes, were the healthcare workers who've been at the frontlines of the pandemic since 2020. Further, Prince Harry and Meghan Markle took the fourth spot, with each of them getting 1.9% of the votes. Harry made headlines around the world earlier this year after he released his memoir Spare. The 2023 TIME100 list will be released on 13 April.

Aaditya Thackeray selected for World Economic Forum's Young Global Leaders Class 2023

The World Economic Forum (WEF) inducted Shiv Sena (UBT) leader Aaditya Thackeray and national vice president of BJP youth wing Madhukeshwar Desai to the list of world's most promising public figures under the age of 40. Tanvi Ratna, Founder and CEO, Policy 4.0. Research Foundation Aakrit Vaish, Co-Founder and CEO, Jio Haptik Technologies Limited Sudarshan Venu, Managing Director, TVS Motor Company Limited Vibin B Joseph, Executive Director and CEO, BiOZEEN are the newest members of its Young Global Leaders Class of 2023. Delhi airport emerges as the world's 9th busiest airport in 2022 According to Airports Council International (ACI) list, Delhi Airport with more than 5.94 crore passenger traffic has become the ninth busiest airport in the world in 2022.

World Energy Transitions: Outlook 2023 report

International Renewable Energy Agency released 'World Energy Transitions : Outlook 2023' report. This report has highlighted that significant progress has been made in the energy transition, particularly in the power sector. According to the report, renewables contributed 83 percent to the global power additions in 2022. As per the report, the deployment of renewables should be increased from 3,000 gigawatt (GW) to 10,000 GW by 2030 to keep the rise of temperature below 1.5 degrees Celsius.

UP bags 3rd position in providing tap water connections in country, beats Rajasthan

Uttar Pradesh superseded Rajasthan and became the third state of the country in terms of number of connections tap water connections under 'Har Ghar Nal Yojana'. Top 5 states providing tap connection include Bihar (1,59,10,093 connections), Maharashtra (1,09,98,678 connections), UP (97,11,717 connections), Gujarat (91,18,449 connections) and Tamil Nadu (79,62,581 connections).

India improves its ranking by 6 spots in global biz environment rankings

India's rank improved by six spots in the global Business Environment Rankings. The Economist Intelligence Unit (EIU) has released the latest Business Environment Rankings (BER), India's rank has improved from 52nd to 46th position. According to the EIU's latest business environment Rankings, Singapore, Canada and Denmark will be the three countries with the best business environment over the next five years. The United States and Switzerland are in the fourth and fifth spot respectively. India ranks 5th in countries with most AI investments India is ranked 5th in the list of countries with the most AI investment as per Stanford University's annual AI Index report. The total amount of investments in AI startups in India was $3.24 billion in 2022. The US, China, UK and Israel are placed ahead of India.

Russia becomes fourth largest import source for India in FY23

Russia has moved up 16 ranks to become the fourth largest import source for India in FY 2022-23, with a 369.4 percent increase (year-on-year) to $46.33 billion, comprising primarily crude and petroleum products, while its share in India's imports expanded to 6.5 per cent from 1.6 per cent in the previous fiscal. The top destinations for Indian exports in FY 2022-23 included the US with exports valued at $78.31 billion, the UAE at $31.33 billion, the Netherlands at $20.90 billion, China at $15.32 billion, Singapore at $11.95 billion, Bangladesh at $11.67 billion and the UK at $11.46 billion.

World of Statistics releases ranking of the world's "most criminal countries"

World of Statistics has shared the ranking of the world's "most criminal countries". On the list, Venezuela has been ranked top, followed by Papua New Guinea (2), Afghanistan (3), South Africa (4), Honduras (5), Trinidad (6), Guyana (7), Syria (8), Somalia (9) and Jamaica (10), respectively. India stood at 77 spots while the US and UK were ahead of India in the criminal ranking country. The USA was at 55th number and the UK at 65th rank , according to the World of Statistics.

US became India's largest trading partner in FY23

The US became India's largest trading partner in FY23. Bilateral trade between both countries has increased by 7.65% to $128.55 billion in 2022-23 as against $119.5 billion in 2021-22 as per provisional data of the commerce ministry. Exports to the US increased by 2.81% to $78.31 billion in 2022-23. During 2022-23, the UAE was India's third largest trading partner with $76.16 billion. UAE was followed by Saudi Arabia ($52.72 billion) and Singapore (USD 35.55 billion). India is the world's 3rd largest consumer market.

Bengaluru tops highest digital transactions in 2022

Bengaluru with 29 million transactions worth USD 65 billion e merged on top in digital payment transactions. New Delhi with 19.6 million transactions worth USD 50 billion and Mumbai with 18.7 million transactions worth USD 49.5 billion are in second and third spots. Pune and Chennai are also among the top 5 in digital payment transactions in 2022.

India is the 4th biggest military spender in the world: SIPRI

India, which has sharpened its focus on building its defence capabilities and strengthening military infrastructure along the China border, was the fourth biggest military spender in the world in 2022 after the United States, China and Russia. Saudi Arabia was in fifth place. The five countries accounted for 63% of the world's military spending. India's military spending of $81.4 billion was the fourth highest in the world. Total global military expenditure increased by 3.7% in 2022, hitting a new high of $2,240 billion, Sipri said while highlighting that Russia's invasion of Ukraine was a major driver of the growth in spending last year.

In 2022, China's military spending reached $292 billion. In February, India set aside Rs. 5.93 lakh crore for defence spending in this year's budget, including a capital outlay of Rs.1.62 lakh crore for the military's modernisation, with the allocation almost 12% higher than that in last year's budget estimates, and about 2% more compared to that in the revised estimates for 2022-23.

Also, India's share of the global arms imports was the highest during the last five years at 11%, followed by Saudi Arabia (9.6%), Qatar (6.4%), Australia (4.7%) and China (4.7%), according to data published by Sipri that measures weapons imports over five-year periods.

About SIRPI

The SIPRI is an independent international institute dedicated to research into conflict, armaments, arms control and disarmament. Established in 1966 at Stockholm, SIPRI provides data, analysis and recommendations, based on open sources, to policymakers, researchers, media and the interested public.

India climbs 6 places on World Bank index to 38 among 139 countries

India has improved its ranking in the World Bank's Logistic Performance Index 2023 by six places , owing to significant investments in both soft and hard infrastructure as well as technology, which has led to animprovement in the country's port performance. Singapore and Finland are the most efficient and highest-ranked LPI countries.

India's ranking: According to the report, India's rank in the index of 139 countries has risen to 38 from 44 in 2018. International shipments : In 2023, India's ranking for international shipments improved significantly, moving up from 44 in 2018 to 22. Logistics competence and equality : The country also climbed four places to rank 48 in logistics competence and equality. Timeline: In terms of timelines, India saw a significant improvement, moving up 17 places in the rankings. Tracking and tracing: Additionally, India improved three places in tracking and tracing, now ranking at 38. The LPI 2023 allows for comparisons across 139 countries.

TCS tops LinkedIn's 2023 Top Companies India list showcasing best places to work

Tata Consultancy Services has emerged as the top company in a list, which showcases the best places to work and grow careers, for 2023. TCS is followed by Amazon (2) and Morgan Stanley (3) in the '2023 Top Companies India' list prepared by LinkedIn. There has been a shift from tech companies, which dominated the list last year, with companies across financial services, oil and gas, professional services, manufacturing and gaming featuring in this year's list. A vast majority of the companies, that is 10 out of 25 comp anies are from the financial services/ banking/ fintech space, including companies such as Macquarie Group (5), HDFC Bank (11), Mastercard (12), and Yubi (14). The 2023 Top Companies India list is based on LinkedIn's data to rank companies on eight pillars that have been shown to lead to career progression, including ability to advance, skills growth, company stability, external opportunity, company affinity, gender diversity, educational background and employee presence in the country.

Karnataka bags national award for Fasal Bima Yojana

Karnataka has bagged the national award for the best implementation of Pradhan Mantri Fasal Bima Yojana (PMFBY), a crop subsidy insurance scheme, for the year 2022-23. The PMFBY is a large-scale crop subsidy insurance scheme aimed to safeguard the farmers, implemented in Karnataka in 2016. This scheme is being managed by the Department of Agriculture, Cooperation and Farmers' Welfare, under the Ministry of Agriculture, along with empanelled general insurance companies. PMFBY is being implemented in Karnataka, through its own portal 'Samrakshane', designed and developed by the state through National Informatics Centre (NIC). The Agriculture and Farmers Welfare Department, Government of Puducherry, has secured the top rank in the smaller States category for its successful implementation of the Pradhan Mantri Fasal Bima Yojana (PMFBY) crop insurance scheme.

Gates named after Sachin Tendulkar, Brian Lara unveiled at Sydney Cricket Ground

The Sydney Cricket Ground (SCG) used legendary Indian cricketer Sachin Tendulkar's 50th birthday celebrations to unveil gates at the iconic Australia venue that are named after the India legend and fellow cricketing great Brian Lara from West Indies. All visiting players will now take the field through the newly-named Lara-Tendulkar Gates, with the duo bestowed with the honour to coincide with Mr. Tendulkar's 50th birthday. Mr. Tendulkar's first Test century on Australia shores came at the picturesque Sydney venue and the champion right-hander averaged a whopping 157 from five Test matches at the ground. The unveiling also took place 30 years after Lara made his famous innings of 277 against Australia at the SCG in 1993 and the West Indies great was thrilled to receive the honour.

Ratan Tata Awarded Australia's Highest Civilian Honour

Tata Sons' Chairman Emeritus Ratan Tata has been conferred with Australia's highest civilian honour, the country's High Commissioner to India Barry O'Farrell announced. The Order of Australia (AO) award was presented for the industrialist's efforts in strengthening the India - Australia bilateral relations. The 85-year-old has batted for the 2022 India-Australia Economic Cooperation and Trade Agreement, while Tata Consultancy Services (TCS) reportedly employs the biggest Australian workforce of any Indian firm with about 17,000 employees. In October 2022, Tata received 'Sewa Ratna' from the RSS-affiliated Sewa Bharti for his philanthropic pursuits. He is also a 2008 recipient of India's second-highest civilian award, the Padma Vibhushan.

Wing Commander Deepika Misra becomes 1st woman IAF officer to get Gallantry Award

Wing Commander Deepika Mishra made history by becoming the first female officer in the Indian Air Force to be honoured with a gallantry award. In 2022, Deepika was among the awardees announced for the Vayu Seva Medal for Gallantry on Independence Day. On April 20, 2023, the medal has been conferred on Deepika by Indian Air Force Chief Air Chief Marshal VR Chaudhari at an investiture ceremony held in New Delhi.

About Deepika Mishra

In August 2021, Deepika Mishra was deployed to conduct humanitarian assistance and disaster relief operations in response to flash floods in northern Madhya Pradesh. She was the first and only responder to reach the affected area and saved the lives of

47 people. IAF chief presented the award to two IAF officers were awarded Yudh Seva Medal, 13 officers, and air warriors received Vayu Sena Medal (Gallantry), 13 officers Vayu Sena Medal and 30 Vishisht Seva Medal.

Angela Merkel received the highest order of Merit of Germany

Former German chancellor Angela M erkel received the highest order of Merit of Germany. She has been honoured with this award for her achievements in office, despite growing criticism of her decisions on Russia and her energy policy. President Frank-Walter Steinmeier handed over her the Grand Cross award. Former chancellors Konrad Adenauer and Helmut Kohl have received this award twice.

About Angela Merkel

Angela Merkel led Germany from 2005 to 2021. She served for four terms. She was the first woman to take the post of chancellor. Germany's Order of Merit is the only federal decoration of Germany. It is given for special achievements in political, economic, cultural, intellectual or honorary fields. It was created by first President of Germany Theodor Heuss in 1951.

Synergy Group wins prestigious Tanker Operator Award

Synergy Group, which operates a fleet of more than 560 vessels, has won the GREEN4SEA Tanker Operator award for its 'leadership role in global tanker management.' Founded in 2006 by Captain Rajesh Unni, the group took home the award through a representative during a hybrid event held in Athens. Instituted by the SAFETY4SEA shipping and maritime news portal, the awards recognise operational excellence and industry leadership in the tanker sector. Capt Rajesh Unni, CEO, Synergy Group.

PM GatiShakti national master plan wins award for excellence in public administration

PM Gati Shakti's national master plan initiative received the award for excellence in public administration. Prime Minister Narendra Modi presented the award for excellence in public administration to PM Gati Shakti national master plan initiative. This award is conferred for excellence in public administration for the effective implementation of priority programmes. This award was instituted to recognise the extraordinary and innovative work done by districts and organisations of the central and state governments for people's welfare. This initiative of Ministry of Commerce a nd Industry has received the award in innovation category.

A GIS enabled national master plan digital platform has also been developed. Data related to land records, ports, forest, schools, railway stations, water bodies, telecom towers, and highways are available on the portal of this initiative. PM Gati Shakti National Master Plan was launched in October 2021. It was launched for the integrated and planned development of critical infrastructure projects to reduce logistics costs. It will help in developing infrastructure in different fields including transport and productivity.

New York City tops the list of world's wealthiest cities 2023

New York City topped a new list of the world's wealthiest cities in 2023, with Japan's Tokyo and Silicon Valley's Bay Area claiming the second and third spots. Mumbai featured at #21 while Delhi, Bengaluru, Kolkata and Hyderabad too found a mention. The list, compiled by London-based consultancy Henley & Partners, ranked the cities by taking into account the number of resident millionaires (rounded off to the neared 1o0) as of December 31, 2022. It was dominated by cities in the United States and China — not one European city featuring in the top 10, with the exception of London. The report included four US cities in the top 10- New York City, The Bay Area, Los Angeles and Chicago. In terms of billionaires, California's Bay Area won as 63 call the region surrounding Silicon Valley and San Francisco home. It was followed by New York, Beijing, Los Angeles and Shanghai.

Bengaluru got a special mention as one of the fastest-growing cities in the Asia Pacific. The report said: "Also known as the "Garden City" and the "Silicon Valley of India", Bengaluru has a booming tech sector." The World's Wealthiest Cities Report 2023 covered 97 cities across the world, using data from wealth intelligence firm, New World Wealth. Mumbai 21st, Delhi 36th, Bengaluru 60th, Kolkata 63rd and Hyderabad 65th.

India retains third spot as a unicorn hub: Hurun report

India has retained its 3rd spot as the country with the highest number of unicorns worldwide after the US and China. With 68 new unicorns, India lags behind the US and China, which have 666 and 316 unicorns, respectively. India added 14 new unicorns since the pandemic began. Despite the rise, none of the start-ups made it to the top 10. According to the report, BYJU's is the top-most unicorn in India, with a valuation of $22 billion, followed by Swiggy and Dream11, valued at $8 billion each.

The report also mentioned that India and China produce more offshore unicorns than any other country. Founders from India co-founded 70 unicorns outside, while China co-founded 32 outside of China, compared with 316 in China. San Francisco retained the title of 'World Unicorn Capital' with 181 unicorns, up 30. New York is in the second spot with 126 unicorns, up 41. With 79 unicorns Beijing was down 12 to the third position, followed by Shanghai with 66. London with 42 unicorns was fifth, followed by Bengaluru and Shenzhen with 33 unicorns each.

India to overtake China as world's most populous countr y by mid-2023: U.N.
India will overtake China as the world's most populous nation by the middle of this year. According to the United Nations Population Fund's World Population Report, India's population is estimated to be 1.4286 billion by mid-year of 2023, compared to 1.4257 billion for China. India's population will be around 3 million more than its neighbour china.

As per the International Monetary Fund, China's per capita income is projected to be 5x India's ($2,601) in 2023. The total population of India was expected to be 1.388 billion in 2023 based on the 2011 census data, according to the report of the Technical Group on Population Projections under the Ministry of Health and Family Welfare presented in July 2020.

MOU and Agreement

Rural Development Ministry inks deal with 19 employers
The Ministry of Rural Development has signed MoUs with 19 'Captive Employers' for the training and placement of 31,000 rural youths under the Deen Dayal Upadhyaya Grameen Kaushalya Yojana (DDUGKY). 'Captive Employers' refer to companies or industries that select rural youths, skill them, and deploy them in one of their own establishments, sister concerns or subsidiaries.

NTPC Renewable Energy Signs Term Sheet With Greenko ZeroC To Supply Round The Clock RE P ower Of 1300 MW Capacity For Its Green Ammonia Plant

NTPC Renewable Energy Ltd, a wholly owned subsidiary of NTPC Green Energy Limited, has signed Term Sheet with Green ko ZeroC Pvt Ltd (A Greenko Group Company) to Supply 1300 MW Round the Clock RE Power for powering Greenko's upcoming Green Ammonia Plant at Kakinada, India. The agreement between the two companies is one of the world's single largest contract for supply of round-the-clock renewable supply for an industrial client.

About Greenko

Greenko, is one of the World's leading Energy Transition and Decarbonization solutions company.

About NTPC

- NTPC Limited, formerly known as National Thermal Power Corporation Limited, is an Indian central public sector undertaking under the ownership of te Ministry of Power.
- Founded: 7 November 1975,
- Headquarters: New Delhi, India.

Vedanta's Hindustan Zinc Limited Signs MoU with RCA to Set up Anil Agarwal

Vedanta's Hindustan Zinc Limited (HZL) signed a memorandum of understanding (MoU) with the Rajasthan Cricket Association (RCA) for the development of world's 3rd largest cricket stadium in the village Chonp in Jaipur. Vedanta's HZL will spend INR 300 crore on the stadium, one of the largest corporate investments in India's sports infrastructure. The stadium will be named "Anil Agarwal International Cricket Stadium, Jaipur". The stadium facilities will be spread across 100 acres and have a seating c apacity of more than 75,000.

RRI signs MoU with Indian Navy for developing secure maritime communications using quantum technologies

The Department of Science and Technology signed a MoU with the Indian Navy for developing secure maritime communications. Under this MoU, the Department of Science and Technology will develop secure maritime communications using Quantum Technology. Raman Research Institute's Quantum Information and Computing (QuIC) lab will lead the project of developing quantum key distribution techniques. QuIC lab is leading India's research in the field of secure quantum communication.

Namami Gange Signs Agreement With 49 Universities To Inspire Youth Towards Water Conservation & River Rejuvenation

The National Mission for Clean Ganga has signed an agreement with 49 universities. The agreement has been signed to inspire youth toward water conservation and river rejuvenation. The aim of the MoU is to bring students at the forefront of the mass movement for creating a sustainable ecosystem of rivers.

Credai, Indian Green Building Council to erect 4,000 projects by 2030

The Confederation of Real Estate Developers Association of India (Credai) has partnered with the Indian Green Building Council (IGBC) to build over 1,000 certified green projects across India in the next two years, and 4,000 projects by 2030. This initiative aligns with India's vision of reaching net-zero by 2070.

NHAI enables FASTag-based payments at tiger reserve

NHAI incorporated company Indian Highways Management Company Limited (IHMCL) signed an MoU with the Nagarjunasagar-Srisailam Tiger Reserve to carry out Electronic Tolling.

Indian Oil & US-based LanzaJet to set up India's first green aviation fuel firm

Indian Oil Corporation is planning to set up a joint venture with US-based clean energy technology company LanzaJet Inc and multiple domestic airlines for production of sustainable aviation fuel (SAF). Through the proposed venture, a plant will be set up to make SAF with alcohol-to-jet technology at IOCL's Panipat refinery in Haryana at a cost of Rs 3,000 crore.

India signs MoU with World Food Programme for sending wheat to Afghanistan

India has signed an MoU with the World Food Programme for sending 10,000 metric tonnes of wheat to the people of Afghanistan. The officials of the Ministry of External Affairs and the United Nations WFP signed a MoU in Mumbai. Recently, the India Central Asia Joint Working Group on Afghanistan announced to send 20,000 MT of wheat through the Iranian port of Chahbahar.

About WFP

World Food Programme (WFP) was founded in December 1961 and is headquartered in Rome, Italy. It is the world's largest humanitarian intergovernmental organization that focuses on hunger and food security. Cindy McCain is the head of WFP.

Tamil Nadu inks pact for Rs 2,302 crore investment with footwear firm

The Tamil Nadu government signed a memorandum of understanding with a well-known footwear maker for an investment of ₹2,302 crore in the state. The MoU was signed with High Glory Footwear, a subsidiary of Taiwan-based Pou Chen Corporation, the world's largest branded footwear manufacturer.

Godrej Agrovet signs MoU with the State Government of Andhra Pradesh

Godrej Agrovet has signed a Memorandum of Understanding (MoU) with the state government on the sidelines of the Andhra Pradesh Global Investors Summit (APGIS) 2023. As a part of the MoU, Godrej Agrovet's oil palm business will be making an estimated investment of Rs 100 crore to set up a manufacturing facility for edible oil refinery and solvent extraction plant. The company already has 45,000 hectare area of oil palm plantation area in Andhra Pradesh (AP). The proposed new plant will have a projected refining capacity of 400 tonnes per day and will be set up in Seethanagaram, Eluru District in AP. This is company's first downstream project for value-added products in oil and fats.

Indian Immunologicals signs MoU with ICAR-CIFA for commercial development of fish vaccine

Indian Immunologicals Limited (IIL) entered into a partnership with the Central Institute of Freshwater Aquaculture (CIFA), Bhubaneswar, an Indian Council of Agricultural Research (ICAR) Institute for the commercial development of vaccines against Hemorrhagic Septicemia, also called Aeromonas Septicemia, Ulcer Disease or Red-Sore Disease in freshwater fish. IIL is the first in India to get fish vaccines. India is the third largest fish producer in the global sphere and more than 65 percent of India's fish is through Inland Fisheries and Aquaculture.

NTPC and Chempolis India to collaborate on Feasibility Study for setting up Bamboo-based Bio-Refinery at Bongaigaon

NTPC Ltd, the largest power-generating utility in India, and Chempolis India, a Fortum group associate company and a Finnish bio-refining technology provider, have signed a Memorandum of Understanding (MoU) to explore the feasibility of setting up a bamboo-based bio-refinery in Assam's Bongaigaon. Chempolis will work with NTPC to conduct the feasibility study for the project which shall utilise bamboo for the production of 2G ethanol, bio-coal for thermal power plant and other value-added products. The bio-coal produced by the bio-refinery shall partly replace coal in the power plant, effectively converting 5 percent of the generation of the power plant to green.

Airtel partners with Secure Meters to deploy NB-IoT in Bihar

Bharti Airtel (Airtel) has partnered with Secure Meters for deploying narrow band (NB-IoT) services that will power 1.3 million homes in Bihar through a smart meter solution. This deployment will be India's first NB-IoT solution on a narrow band with a fall-back option that will work on 2G and 4G and ensure real-time connectivity and uninterrupted transfer of critical data. NB-IoT is a low-power, wide area, radio network technology developed by 3GPP which enables a wide variety of IoT devices and services including smart meters. Airtel's NB-IoT platform is future-ready and is scalable to 5G, the company said adding that the NB-IoT proposition also includes its advanced IoT platform 'The Airtel IoT Hub' which has been customised to suit the needs of advance metering infrastructure service providers (AMISPs).

Air India signs multi-year global distribution services partnership with US-based Sabre Corporation

Air India announced a new multi-year global distribution services partnership with US-based Sabre Corporation. The collaboration enables travel agents and corporations around the world to access Air India fares and seats through Sabre's extensive global travel marketplace. In addition to the distribution services, Air India said it is utilising Sabre's consultancy expertise to help determine optimal routes for its existing and new fleet. Air India earlier this year announced placing a 470 aircraft order with Boeing and Airbus. This long-term global distribution partnership will support our ambitious growth plans while paving the ground for the airline's transition towards a more dynamic, merchandising-focused model.

About Air India

- Air India is the flag carrier of India, headquartered in New Delhi.
- It is owned by Talace Private Limited, a fully owned subsidiary of Tata Sons, after Air India Limited's former owner, the Government of India, completed the sale.
- CEO: Campbell Wilson.

IIT Roorkee signs pact with Taiwanese centre for developing tech solutions for earthquakes, floods

Indian Institute of Technology Roorkee (IIT Roorkee) and the National Science and Technology Centre for Disaster Reduction (NCDR), Taiwan have signed an agreement with an aim to develop technology solutions to natural hazards, including earthquakes, landslides, floods, debris flow, and compound disasters. The researchers aim to co-establish an early warning sensor network equipped with P-Alert sensors at selected locations in Uttarakhand. The signing ceremony was followed by a technical workshop on Earthquake Early Warning Systems (EEWS). India's first Earthquake Early Warning System (EEWS), namely Uttarakhand Earthquake Early Warning System (UEEWS), is established at the IIT Roorkee. At present, the alert system is active only within Uttarakhand, India.

CSIR signs an Umbrella MoU with OIL India

The Council of Scientific and Industrial Research (CSIR), New Delhi and Oil India Ltd. (OIL), a Navaratna NOC inked an umbrella Memorandum of Understanding (MoU) to pursue technological partnership in select domains across the Energy value chain. This will be a collaborative arrangement between labs of CSIR and OIL. The objective of the MoU is to facilitate collaboration for pursuing research in advanced technologies for energy security. Oil India Limited is a central public sector undertaking under the ownership of the Ministry of Petroleum and Natural Gas, Government of India. Headquarters: Noida, Dr. Ranjit Rath- Chairman & Managing Director.

Mitsubishi Electric to set up $222-million AC manufacturing plant in Chennai

Mitsubishi Electric India has signed an agreement with Mahindra Industrial Park Chennai Ltd , a joint venture between Mahindra World City Developers and Japan's Sumitomo Corporation, to set up an airconditioners and compressors manufacturing plant at Origins by Mahindra, Chennai. The electric and electronic equipment manufacturing company will invest around $222 million (about ₹1,819 crore) in the facility spread over 52 acres. According to a regulatory filing by Mahindra Lifespace Developers Ltd, the plant will be operational by October 2025. Kazuhiko Tamura is a Managing Director of Mitsubishi Electric India Pvt Ltd.

India, Thailand to explore mutual recognition pacts for nursing, accountancy, medical tourism

India and Thailand have agreed to explore mutual recognition/ cooperation arrangements (MRAs) in nursing, accounting, audio-visual and medical tourism, in a meeting of the India Thailand Joint Trade Committee (JTC) in New Delhi. The two sides discussed the scope for collaboration in the services sector and agreed to work on possible MRAs in key sectors. MRAs aim to facilitate mobility of professionals with countries that sign such a pact, agreeing to recognise qualifications earned by professionals in the partner countries. Thailand is India's important trading partner in the 10-member ASEAN with total trade of $16.89 billion in 2022-23. It accounts for 13.6 per cent of India's total trade with the ASEAN. Thailand is an important destination for India's gems and jewellery, mechanical machinery, auto and auto components and agricultural products, especially marine products.

Science & Technology

ISRO releases images of Earth captured by its EOS-06 satellite

The Indian Space Research Organisation (ISRO) has released images of Earth captured by the Earth Observation satellite (EOS-6) satellite. The images are a mosaic generated by the ISRO's National Remote Sensing Centre (NRSC). NRSC/ISRO has generated a global False Colour Composite (FCC) mosaic from the images captured by the Ocean Colour Monitor (OCM) payload on board EOS-06. Mosaic with 1 km spatial resolution is generated by combining 2939 individual images, after processing 300 GB data to show the Earth as seen during February 1 and 15.

About ISRO

- Founded : 15 August 1969
- Headquarters : Bangalore, Karnataka, India
- Chairman : Sreedhara Somanath
- The ISRO is the national space agency of India, & it operates under the Department of Space (DOS).

Nokia to launch 4G mobile network on the moon in late 2023

Nokia has announced plans to launch a 4G mobile network on the moon. This initiative is in collaboration with National Aeronautics and Space Administration (NASA), and the 4G mobile network will be launched in a SpaceX rocket near the end of 2023. To improve communication capabilities and provide relief to astronauts during their missions while also enhancing lunar discoveries.

About Nokia

- Established : 1865
- Headquarters: Espoo, Finland.
- Nokia Corporation is a Finnish multinational telecommunications, information technology, and consumer electronics corporation.

Bharat Dynamics Limited Successfully Test Fires 3rd Generation Man-portable Anti Tank Guided Missile - Amogha-II

The Bharat Dynamics Limited (BDL) has successfully conducted a field firing test of its latest 3rd generation man-portable Anti Tank Guided Missile (ATGM), Amogha-III. This indigenous missile has been developed under Integrated Guided Missile Development Programme (IGMDP).

About BDL

- Founded : 1970
- Headquarters :Hyderabad, Telangana, India
- Chairman & Managing Director : Commodore Siddharth Mishra

Indian Immunologicals signs MoU with ICAR-CIFA for fish vaccine development

Hyderabad based Indian Immunologicals Limited (IIL) entered into a partnership with the Central Institute of Freshwater Aquaculture (CIFA), Bhubaneswar, an Indian Council of Agricultural Research (ICAR) Institute for the commercial development of vaccines against Hemorrhagic Septicemia, also called Aeromonas Septicemia, Ulcer Disease or Red-Sore Disease in freshwater fish. Currently there are no fish vaccines available in India on a commercial scale to prevent aquaculture infections.

Amazon to launch first of 3,000 internet satellites to space in 2024

Amazon.com plans to launch its first internet satellites to space in the first half of 2024 as it prepares to vie with Elon Musk's SpaceX and others to provide broadband internet globally. Amazon's satellite internet unit, Project Kuiper, will begin mass-producing the satellites later 2023.

Skyroot Aerospace Successfully Test Fired 3D-Printed Cryogenic Engine — Dhawan-II

The private space vehicle company Skyroot Aerospace has test-fired its 3D-printed Dhawan II engine for a duration of 200 seconds in Telangana. The test was conducted at Solar Industries propulsion test facility in Nagpur, Maharashtra using Skyroot's indigenously developed mobile cryogenic engine test pad.

About Skyroot Aerospace

- Founded : 12 June 2018
- Headquarters : Hyderabad, Telangana, India
- CEO : Pawan Kumar Chandana

ISRO successfully conducts landing experiment of the Reusable Launch Vehicle

The Indian Space Research Organisation (ISRO) successfully carried out the landing experiment of the Reusable Launch Vehicle-Technology Demonstration (RLV-TD) programme at the Aeronautical Test Range in Challakere, Karnataka. The RLV took off by a Chinook Helicopter of the Indian Air Force (IAF) as an underslung load and flew to a height of 4.5 km (above Mean sea level MSL). ISRO conducted the first experimental mission of its Reusable Launch Vehicle – Technology Demonstrator (RLV-TD) on May 23, 2016, from Satish Dhawan Space Centre, Sriharikota.

NASA Names 4 Astronauts to Next Moon Mission - Artemis II lunar Mission

The National Aeronautics and Space Administration (NASA) and the Canadian Space Agency (CSA) announced the 4 astronauts crew for the Artemis II mission which includes 3 American nationals and 1 Canadian astronaut. Artemis II mission is a mission to explore more areas of the moon. The 10-day Artemis II mission will test the agency's powerful Space Launch System rocket as well as the life-support systems aboard the Orion spacecraft. Artemis II is expected to reach a point more than 230,000 miles (370,000 km) away from the Earth. It will be launched from the Kennedy Space Center in Florida using the SLS rocket. Artemis I mission was successfully completed in December 2022.

Kenya Space Agency to launch its first operational Satellite

The Kenya Space Agency (KSA) is set to launch its first operational Earth observation satellite "Taifa-1" or "Nation-1" in Swahili, on April 10, 2023. The launch is in partnership with SpaceX & the satellite will be on board its Falcon 9 rocket from Vandenberg Base in California in the United States of America (USA).

About Kenya

- President- William Ruto
- Prime Minister- Raila Odinga
- Capital- Nairobi
- Currency- Kenyan Shilling(KES)

China's Space Pioneer launched first liquid-fueled commercial rocket Tianlong-2 into orbit

The Chinese space startup 'Space Pioneer (also known as Beijing Tianbing Technology Company Limited)successfully launched 'Tianlong-2 rocket (TL-2) into orbit from China's Jiuquan Satellite Launch Centerlocated in the Gobi Desert, Inner Mongolia. This is the first time that a liquid fueled rocket was launched into orbit by a Chinese aerospace company. Also, it was the first time that a startup company Space Pioneer successfully reached orbit on its first attempt.

About China

- President : Xi Jinping
- Capital : Beijing
- Currency : Renminbi

Twitter's iconic blue bird logo replaced with 'Doge' meme of Dogecoin blockchain and cryptocurrency

- The classic blue bird logo of the social media giant Twitter, has been replaced with the "doge" meme.
- The 'doge' meme has the face of a Shiba Inu.

About Twitter, Inc

- Founded : March 21, 2006
- Headquarters : San Francisco, California, United States
- CEO :Elon Musk

Iran successfully tests homemade kamikaze drone equipped with 50 kg warhead

Iran's Islamic Revolution Guards Corps (IRGC) has successfully tested a homemade long-range, highprecision kamikaze drone named Meraj-532, equipped with a 50-kg warhead. It is a kamikaze drone equipped with a piston engine. It has a range of 450 km. It is capable of flying at a maximum altitude of 12,000 feet for three straight hours. It has a 50-kg warhead and can be assembled and prepared for flight easily, making it suitable for rapid reaction operations.

Unique Identification Authority of India- IIT Bombay join hands to develop touchless biometric capture system

The Unique Identification Authority of India (UIDAI) signed a memorandum of understanding (MoU) with the Indian Institute of Technology, Bombay (IIT-Bombay), to develop a touchless biometric capture system for easier use, anytime and anywhere. Under the MoU, UIDAI and IIT Bombay will carry out joint research to build a mobile capture system for fingerprints along with a liveness model integrated with the capture system. The NCETIS is a joint initiative by IIT Bombay and the Ministry of Electronics and Information Technology (MeitY), under its flagship Digital India Programme.

About UIDAI

- Headquarters : New Delhi, Delhi
- CEO : Saurabh Garg
- It is a statutory authority established under the provisions of the Aadhaar (Targeted Delivery of Financial and Other Subsidies, Benefits and Services) Act, 2016 ("Aadhaar Act 2016") in 2016 under the Ministry of Electronics and Information Technology (MeitY).

About IIT Bombay

- Established : 1958
- Headquarters : Mumbai, Maharashtra, India
- Chairman : Dr. Sharad Kumar Saraf

About MeitY

- Cabinet Minister : Ashwini Vaishnaw
- Minister of State : Rajeev Chandrasekhar

Drone start-up Garuda Aerospace becomes first to receive agri drone subsidy

Chennai-based drone startup Garuda Aerospace Private Limited has become the first company to receive the government's agri-drone subsidy for the agricultural drones. This subsidy is part of the Indian government's efforts to promote the use of agricultural drones. Garuda Kisan Drones were given to 8 farmers under the Agri-drone subsidy at an event held in Pune,Maharashtra. This subsidy is just one of many initiatives launched by the Union government to support the development of India's drone industry. This will benefit farmers not only by making their jobs easier and more efficient, but it will also help to increase agricultural productivity and reduce food waste.

About Garuda Aerospace Private Limited

- Established : 2015
- Headquarters : Chennai, Tamil Nadu
- CEO : Agnishwar Jayaprakash

European Space Agency set to launch Jupiter Icy Moons Explorer

The European Space Agency (ESA) is all set to launch the Jupiter Icy Moons Explorer, or Juice, mission from its spaceport in French Guiana on an Ariane 5 launcher. ESA's Juice mission will make detailed observations of gas giant Jupiter and its 3 large ocean-bearing moons - Ganymede, Callisto and Europa.

Elena Geo Systems launches NavIC chip to reduce dependence on GPS

Elena Geo Systems, a Bengaluru-based space technology company, launched Indigenous Navigation with Indian Constellation (NavIC) chip at the Defence Space Symposium, to reduce dependence on the American Global Positioning System (GPS).

Russia conducts test launch of 'advanced' intercontinental ballistic missile

The Russian defence ministry has conducted the successful test launch of an "advanced" intercontinental ballistic missile (ICBM). The missile was launched from the Kapustin Yar test site in Russia's southern Astrakhan region.

Purpose

To test advanced combat equipment of intercontinental ballistic missiles.

About Russia

- President : Vladimir Putin
- Prime Minister : Mikhail Mishustin
- Capital : Moscow
- Currency : Ruble

Kenya successfully launches first operational satellite Taifa-1 into space onboard SpaceX Falcon-9 rocket

Kenya successfully launched its first operational earth observation satellite, 'Taifa-1 satellite,' into orbit. The launch took place on a SpaceX rocket Falcon-9 from the Vandenberg Base in California, United States (US).

Key Statistics

- Egypt was the first African country to send a satellite into space in 1998.
- In 2018, Kenya launched its first experimental nanosatellite from the International Space Station (ISS).

About Kenya

- President : William Ruto
- Capital : Nairobi
- Currency : Kenyan shilling

NASA's Lucy Spacecraft Spots Jupiter's Trojan Asteroids for the First Time

NASA's asteroid-hunting spacecraft, Lucy, captured its first views of four Jupiter Trojan asteroids that are thought to be leftover from the formation of the solar system.

About Lucy Mission

It was launched by NASA from the Cape Canaveral Space Force Station in Florida in 2021. It is a 12-year mission which will take close observations of nine of Jupiter's Trojans and two main belt asteroids along with that. It is the first spacecraft sent to study the Trojan asteroids, which orbit the Sun in the same path that the planet Jupiter takes.

Türkiye launches its largest warship and world's first drone carrier - TCG Anadolu

Turkish President Mr Recep Tayyip Erdogan unveiled Türkiye's largest warship and the world's first unmanned combat aerial vehicle (UCAV) carrier, TCG Anadolu, has been delivered to the country's navy.

About Türkiye

- President : Recep Tayyip Erdoğan
- Capital : Ankara
- Currency : Turkish lira

North Korea Tests Second Underwater Drone 'Haeil-2'

To show off its strength against the United States of America (USA) and South Korea's giant military exercise, North Korea tested its second nuclear-capable underwater attack drone “Haeil-2" test. The Haeil-2" test was carried out in Kajin Port, Kumya Country, South Hamgyong Province.

About North Korea

- President : Kim Jong Un
- Capital : Pyongyang
- Currency : Korean People's won

IIT Indore in collaboration with NASA-Caltech develops low-cost camera for multispectral imaging of flame

The Indian Institute of Technology (IIT) Indore in collaboration with NASA-Caltech from the United States (US) and Sweden’s University of Gothenburg has developed a low-cost camera setup which can provide multispectral imaging of 4 chemical species in a flame using a single DSLR camera. The low-cost DSLR camera device named “CL-Flam” has been developed after 3 years’ research.

NISAR satellite to map Himalayas’ seismic zones

The Indian Space Research Organization (ISRO) and the US National Aeronautics and Space Administration (NASA) have jointly developed the NISAR (NASA-ISRO Synthetic Aperture Radar) satellite. The forthcoming satellite will map the most earthquake-prone regions in the Himalayas with unprecedented regularity. The data it will generate could potentially provide advance warning of landslides, as seen recently in Joshimath, Uttarakhand, as well as pinpoint locations most at risk from earthquakes.

Key Highlights

The cost of the NISAR satellite is expected to be around $900 million (with ISRO contributing about onetenth). It will use two frequency bands: L-band and S-band to photograph the seismically active Himalayan region, creating a "deformation map" every 12 days. These 2 frequency bands will simultaneously provide high-resolution, all-weather data from the satellite, which is expected to follow a Sun-synchronous orbit.

NASA successfully extracts oxygen from lunar soil simulant

The National Aeronautics and Space Administration (NASA) scientists have successfully extracted oxygen from simulated lunar soil. This was the first time that this extraction has been done in a vacuum environment, paving the way for astronauts to one day extract and use resources in a lunar environment, called in-situ resource utilisation. Lunar soil refers to the fine-grained material covering the Moon's surface.

Key Highlights

NASA's Carbothermal Reduction Demonstration (CaRD) team at Johnson Space Center in Houston conducted the test in conditions similar to those found on the Moon by using a special spherical chamber with a 15-feet diameter called the Dirty Thermal Vacuum Chamber. The chamber is considered "dirty" because unclean samples can be tested inside. A carbothermal reactor is where the process of heating and extracting the oxygen takes place.

Japanese Startup Ispace Prepares for World's First Private Lunar Landing

Japanese start-up, ispace inc, is preparing to land its Hakuto-R Mission 1 (M1) spacecraft on the moon in what would be the world's first lunar landing by a private company if it succeeds. The M1 lander is set to touch down after taking off from Cape Canaveral, Florida, on a SpaceX rocket in December. In one of the biggest blows, Japan Aerospace Exploration Agency (JAXA) in March 2023 lost its new medium-lift H3 rocket to forced manual destruction after it reached space. That was less than 5 months since JAXA's solid-fuel Epsilon rocket failed after launch in October.

Key Highlights

The 2.3-metre-tall (7.55 ft) M1 will begin an hour-long landing phase from its current position, in the moon's orbit some 100 km above the surface moving at nearly 6,000 km/hour (3,700 mph). Only the United States, the former Soviet Union, and China have soft-landed a spacecraft on the moon, with attempts in recent years by India and a private Israeli company ending in failure.

After reaching the landing site at the edge of Mare Frigoris, in the moon's northern hemisphere, the M1 is to deploy a two-wheeled, baseball-sized rover developed by JAXA, Japanese toymaker, Tomy Co, Sony Group, and United Arab Emirates' four-wheeled "Rashid" Rover. The M1 is also carrying an experimental solid-state battery made by NGK Spark Plug Co, among other objects to gauge how they perform on the moon. In its second mission scheduled in 2024, the M1 will bring ispace's own rover, while from 2025, it is set to work with U.S. space lab, Draper, to bring NASA payloads to the moon, targeting building a permanently staffed lunar colony by 2040.

ISRO's PSLV-C55 successfully places 2 Singapore satellites into orbit

The Indian Space Research Organisation's (ISRO) successfully launched the Polar Satellite Launch Vehicle C55 (PSLV-C55) mission carrying 2 Singaporean satellites TeLEOS-2 and Lumelite-4 from Satish Dhawan Space Center at Sriharikota in Andhra Pradesh (AP) into a low-earth orbit. At the end of a 22.5 hour countdown, the 44.4 metre tall rocket lifted off majestically from the first launch pad at the pre-fixed at the Satish Dhawan Space Centre, located about 135 km from Chennai.

About TeLEOS-2

TeLEOS-2 is a synthetic aperture radar satellite developed under a partnership between Defence Science and Technology Agency (DSTA), representing the Government of Singapore and ST Engineering. After deployment of the satellite into the about 586 km orbit, it would be used to support the satellite imagery requirements of various agencies within the Government of Singapore. It would be used to provide all-weather day and night coverage and is capable of imaging at one metre full polarimetric resolution for Singapore.

About Lumelite-4

The co-passenger satellite is Lumelite-4, co-developed by the Institute for Infocomm Research and Satellite TEchnology and Research Centre of the National University of Singapore. It is an advanced 12U satellite developed for the technological demonstration of the High-Performance Space-borne VHF data Exchange System

(VDES). This mission follows the successful deployment of the TeLEOS-1 satellite in a PSLV-C29 rocket along with 5 other satellites of Singapore in December 2015.

SpaceX Starship, world's biggest rocket, explodes during first flight test

SpaceX's Starship Spacecraft created history, as the most powerful & biggest rocket ever built lifted off on its first test flight. It was blasted off from Starbase, the SpaceX spaceport in Boca Chica, Texas. The Starship capsule had been scheduled to separate from the first-stage rocket booster 3 minutes into the flight but separation failed to occur and the rocket blew up. The vehicle experienced multiple engines out during the flight test, lost altitude, and began to tumble. The flight termination system was commanded on both the booster and ship. It is standard procedure to destroy a wayward rocket to prevent damage to people or property below. The US space agency National Aeronautics and Space Administration (NASA) has picked Starship to ferry astronauts to the Moon in late 2025 for the first time since the Apollo programme ended in 1972. Starship comprises a 164-ft tall craft for crew and cargo, placed on top of a 230-ft-tall first-stage Super Heavy booster rocket.

IIT Madras Scientists develop an 'Easy-to-use Screening Device for reliable assessment of Blood Vessel Health

Researchers at the Indian Institute of Technology-Madras (IIT-M) developed a device called 'ARTSENS' to assess the health and age of blood vessels and thereby provide early screening for cardiovascular diseases.

Research Team

The research was led by Dr. Jayaraj Joseph, Assistant Professor, Department of Electrical Engineering, IIT Madras.

About 'ARTSENS'

It is a novel, non-invasive device. It can be used in routine medical examinations by even non-experts, to assess and predict vascular health. It is powered by a proprietary non-imaging probe and an intelligent computing platform and is developed by the Healthcare Technology Innovation Centre (HTIC) at IIT Madras.

Solar Industries to supply UAV 'Nagastra' to Indian Army

Solar Industries India Limited, Nagpur, Maharashtra had bagged an order to supply the 400 unmanned aerial vehicle (UAV) 'Nagastra'-I to the Indian Army, beating competitors from Israel and Poland. With government's initiative to bring Atmanirbharta in ammunition and defence systems, the first indigenous Loiter Munition (LM), Nagastra–1, has been designed and developed by Economics Explosives Ltd (EEL), a 100% subsidiary of Solar Industries Nagpur, in association with Z-Motion, Bangalore. A model of 'Nagastra -1' loitering munition was recently displayed in the Army Commanders conference held in New Delhi.

About Nagastra -1

Nagastra -1 having an indigenous content of more than 75% has many world class features. In a 'Kamikaze mode' it can neutralise any hostile threat with Global Positioning Sys tem (GPS) enabled precision strike with an accuracy of 2 m. The fixed wing electric UAV has an endurance of 60 min with a man-in-loop range of 15 km and autonomous mode range of 30 km. In addition to day-night surveillance cameras the loiter munition is equipped with a fragmentation warhead to defeat soft-skin targets. In case a target is not detected or if the mission is aborted, the loiter munition can be called back and made a soft landing with a parachute recovery mechanism enabling it to be reused multiple times.

China launches Fengyun-3G, first satellite dedicated to monitoring heavy rainfalls

China successfully launched Fengyun-3G into space, its first satellite dedicated to measuring precipitation, especially heavy rainfalls during catastrophic weather in global regions of low- and midlatitude, which could provide a powerful tool for monitoring and forecasting of global meteorological disasters. It was launched by China's Long March 4B rocket from the Jiuquan Satellite Launch Center in Northwest China's Gansu Province. It is one of only three such satellites in the world.

About Fengyun-3G

With a lifespan of 6 years i.e. 2023-2029 , the FY-3G is developed by an institute of China Aerospace Science and Technology Corporation (CASC), and its ground system will be built and operated by the China Meteorological Administration (CMA). It can provide information on the 3D structure of precipitation in the Earth's low- and mid-latitude regions. The satellite can accurately sense minute changes in precipitation intensity in the atmosphere, such as the intensity of drizzle at 0.2 millimeters per hour.

After the launch, the satellite observation data in China's global weather prediction model can have an update every 4 hours with a 3-percent increase in accuracy. While the efficiency of monitoring meteorological disasters can be doubled. China currently has eight Fengyun meteorological satellites in orbit, providing data and services to 126 countries and regions.

ISRO to launch Singaporean satellite TeLEOS-2 on the PSLV rocket

The Indian Space Research Organisation (ISRO) is preparing to launch a Singaporean Earth Observation satellite named TeLEOS-2 on April 22, 2023. The satellite will be launched aboard ISRO's Polar Satellite Launch Vehicle (PSLV), from the Satish Dhawan Space Centre in Sriharikota, Andhra Pradesh (AP). This launch will be the PSLV's 55th mission.

What is TeLEOS-2?

ISRO launched TeLEOS-1 in 2015. TeLEOS-1 was the first Singapore commercial Earth Observation Satellite. It was developed by ST Engineering and it will provide imagery which will be used for hotspot monitoring and haze management, along with assistance in aviation accidents, search and rescue operations TeLEOS-2 is a 750kg earth observation satellite that has synthetic aperture radar capable of providing data in 1-metre resolution. It was launched into a low Earth orbit for remote sensing applications. It features synthetic aperture radar which can provide data in 1-metre resolution. ISRO has till now launched 9 satellites from Singapore. The PSLV-C55 is ISRO's 3rd launch this year.

Acquisition and Mergers

LIC increases stake in BATA India Ltd

Life Insurance Corporation (LIC) has increased its shareholding in BATA India. LIC's shareholding has jumped from 57,48,071 to 64,36,692 Equity Shares increasing its shareholding from 4.472% to 5.008% of the paid-up capital. The holding in the LIC crossed 5% and the acquisition of shares were done during the period from Jan 2022 to Mar 2023 at an average cost of INR 1569.33.

About LIC

- Founded : September 1956
- Headquarters : Mumbai, Maharashtra, India

- Chairperson : Siddharth Mohanty

Adani Ports & APSEZ acquires Karaikal Port for Rs 1,485 Cr

The National Company Law Tribunal has approved the acquisition of Karaikal Port (KPPL) by the Adani Ports and Special Economic Zone (APSEZ), the largest transport utility in India. Earlier, APSEZ was declared as the successful resolution applicant under the Corporate Insolvency Resolution Process (CIRP) of KPPL. The amount considered for the acquisition is ₹1,485 crore ($181.2 million).

About APSEZ

- Founded : 26 May 1998
- Headquarters : Ahmedabad, Gujarat, India
- Chairman & MD : Gautam Adani
- CEO : Karan Adani

CCI approves acquisition of certain shareholding of BTS Investment & Bodhi Tree Systems VCC by NBC Universal Media

The Competition Commission of India (CCI) approves the acquisition of certain shareholding of BTS Investment 1 Pte. Ltd. (BTS Investment) & Bodhi Tree Systems VCC (BTS VCC) (Targets) by NBC Universal Media, LLC (NBC Universal) (Acquirer) a wholly-owned subsidiary of Comcast Corporation under Section 31(1) of the Competition Act, 2002.

About CCI

- Established : 14 October 2003
- Headquarters : New Delhi, Delhi, India
- Chairman : Sangeeta Verma
- Secretary : P K Singh
- The CCI is the chief national competition regulator in India.
- It is a statutory body within the Ministry of Corporate Affairs .

CCI approves acquisition of stake in Mukand Sumi Special Steel Limited by Jamnalal Sons Private Limited from Mukand Limited

The Competition Commission of India (CCI) approves acquisition of 5.51% of the equity share capital in Mukand Sumi Special Steel Limited (MSSSL) by Jamnalal Sons Private Limited (JSPL) (Acquirer) from Mukand Limited (Mukand).

Monetary Authority Of Singapore Clears Merger Of HDFC Investments With HDFC Bank

HDFC Bank stated that the Monetary Authority of Singapore (MAS) has given approval for the merger of HDFC Investments Limited and HDFC Holdings Limited with parent HDFC Ltd. As part of a composite scheme of amalgamation, Griha Pte, a wholly-owned subsidiary of HDFC Investments and a foreign step-down subsidiary of HDFC Ltd., received approval for the merger with HDFC Bank.

Key Highlights

The acquisition would result in the bank acquiring 20% or more of the issued share capital of Griha Pte. The proposed amalgamation is subject to receipt of final approvals from the Securities and Exchange Board of India (Sebi) in respect of change in control of certain subsidiaries of HDFC Ltd. This approval will help pave the way for the merger of HDFC and HDFC Bank, expected to be finalised by the third quarter of this financial year. The proposed entity will have a combined asset base of around Rs 18 lakh crore.

Godrej Consumer Products Limited acquires Raymond's FMCG business for Rs 2,825 crore

Godrej Consumer Products Limited (GCPL) will acquire the FMCG business of Raymond Consumer Care Limited (RCCL) for ₹2,825 crore. Both the brands—Park Avenue and KamaSutra are under Raymond Consumer Care, which is a stepdown unit of the Singhania-family owned Raymond, known for its shirting and lifestyle business. Raymond has two fundamental businesses: lifestyle and real estate. Its revenue from FY22 was ₹4,260.66 crore. GCPL is expanding its play in the consumer & earlier, it had acquired Bblunt.

About Godrej Consumer Products Ltd

- Founded : 2001
- Headquarters : Mumbai, Maharashtra, India
- Chairman & Managing Director : Mr. Nadir Godrej
- MD & CEO : Sudhir Sitapati
- Godrej Consumer Products Limited is an Indian consumer goods company.

Hindujas Get In-Principal Approval To Raise Stake In IndusInd Bank

Hinduja Group, Promoters of India's IndusInd Bank have received in-principal approval from the country's central bank Reserve Bank of India (RBI) to increase their stake in IndusInd Bank. The promoters have filled out a form to increase the stake and the due diligence process takes about 90-180 days as per the Reserve Bank of India (RBI) norms. IndusInd's promoters currently hold a stake of about 16.5% in the bank. In 2021, the RBI raised the cap on the stake promoters can hold in a bank to 26% from 15%. IndusInd International Holdings Ltd, an entity belonging to promoters Hinduja Group, have a 12.57% stake in the lender, while IndusInd Ltd has a 3.93% stake as per the company's latest shareholding pattern available with the Indian stock exchange BSE.

CCI Approves Acquisition of Blackstone-Emerson Electric Co by BCP Emerald Aggregator LP

The Competition Commission of India (CCI) has granted its approval for the stake acquisition in climate technologies' business of Emerson Electric Co by BCP Emerald Aggregator LP. The deal has been cleared under the green channel route. BCP Emerald Aggregator LP is an affiliate of United States (US)-based alternative asset manager Blackstone. The CCI has also approved the proposed investment by Stamford Bridge Investment Pte Ltd, an Special Purpose Vehicle (SPV) of GIC (Ventures) and Platinum Falcon B 2018 RSC Ltd (Platinum), in BCP Emerald Aggregator LP. GIC (Ventures) is a subsidiary of Singapore's sovereign wealth fund GIC, while Platinum is an affiliate of the Abu Dhabi Investment Authority (ADIA).

Defence News

10th Edition of Indian – Sri Lanka bilateral maritime exercise SLINEX-2023 The 10th Edition of Indian Navy(IN)- Sri Lanka Navy(SLN) bilateral maritime exercise SLINEX-2023 is scheduled at Colombo, Sri Lanka from 03 - 08 April 2023. The exercise is being conducted in two phases: the Harbour Phase from 03-05 April 2023, Colombo, Sri Lanka followed by a Sea Phase from 06-08 April 2023, Colombo.

About MoD

- Defence Minister : Rajnath Singh
- Minister of State : Ajay Bhatt
- Defence Secretary : Giridhar Aramane

India & U.S. air exercise 'Cope India' begins

The Indian Air Force (IAF) and the US Air Force (USAF) are set to conduct the Cope India exercise from April 10 to 21,2023 at the Kalaikunda airbase in West Bengal. The Japanese Air Self Defence Force (JASDF) participated in Cope India as an observer for the first time in December 2018 based on the Agreement of Defence Ministerial Meeting on August 20, 2018. The IAF is set to field its frontline fighters SU-30MKI, Rafale and the indigenous Light Combat Aircraft along with force multipliers, while the U.S. Air Force is expected to bring in F-15 fighter jets. The last edition of the exercise was held in 2019.

Ministry of Defence signs 3 defence contracts worth ₹5,400 cr for Indian Army & Navy

The Ministry of Defence (MoD) has signed 3 contracts at a total cost of nearly 5400 crore for Indian Army (IA) & Indian Navy (IN) under Buy (Indian – IDMM (Indigenously Designed Developed and Manufactured) category to bolster the defence capabilities of India.

Indian Coast Guard Conducts Regional Search And Rescue (SAR) Exercise in Kakinada, Andhra Pradesh

The Indian Coast Guard (ICG) conducted Regional Search and Rescue (SAR) exercise during 28-29 March 2023 at Kakinada, Andhra Pradesh (AP). To simulate a real time maritime distress scenario and highlight the functioning of SAR organisation for a mass rescue operation. The exercise involved all stakeholders with effective use of available resources towards M-SAR (Maritime Search and Rescue) contingency efficiently. The exercise simulated an Offshore Support vessel (OSV) carrying more than hundreds of passengers that reported a distress call of major fire onboard off Kakinada.

About ICG

- Founded: 1 February 1977
- Headquarters : New Delhi, Delhi, India
- Director General : Virender Singh Pathania
- Motto : Vayam Rakṣāmaḥ means We protect

Ministry of Defence signs Rs 19,600 cr contracts for 11 Next Generation Offshore Patrol Vessels and 6 Next Generation Missile Vessels for Indian Navy

The Ministry of Defence (MoD) signed contracts with Indian shipyards for acquisition of 11 Next Generation Offshore Patrol Vessels (NGOPV) and 6 Next Generation Missile Vessels (NGMV) at an overall cost of approx. Rs 19,600 crore, in a huge boost to achieve 'Aatmanirbharta' in defence,

Ministry of Defence inks Rs 1,700 crore deal with BrahMos Aerospace Private Limited

Ministry of Defence (MoD) inked a contract with BrahMos Aerospace Private Limited (BAPL) for procurement of Next Generation Maritime Mobile Coastal Batteries (Long range) {NGMMCB (LR)} and BrahMos Missiles at an approximate cost of over Rs 1,700 crore under Buy (Indian) Category. The delivery of NGMMCBs is scheduled to commence from 2027. These systems will be equipped with supersonic BrahMos Missiles and will significantly enhance multi-directional maritime strike capability of the Indian Navy. This contract is going to give further boost to indigenous production of critical weapon systems and ammunition with active participation of indigenous industries. This project will generate an employment of more than 90,000 man-days over a period of 4 years.

About BAPL

- Founded : 12 February 1998
- Headquarters : New Delhi, India
- MD & CEO : Shri Atul Dinkar Rane
- BrahMos Aerospace is an Indo-Russian multinational aerospace and defense corporation.
- It was founded as a joint venture (JV) between India's Defence Research and Development Organisation and NPO Mashinostroyenia of Russia.

Defence Ministry signs contract with Bharat Electronics Limited for 13 Lynx-U2 Fire Control Systems for Indian Navy worth Rs 1700 cr

The Ministry of Defence (MoD) signed a contract with Bharat Electronics Limited (BEL), Bangalore, Karnataka for procurement of 13 Lynx-U2 Fire Control Systems for Indian Navy at a total cost of over Rs 1,700 crore under Buy {Indian – IDMM (Indigenously Designed Developed and Manufactured)} category.

Indian Navy conducts offshore security exercise 'Prashthan'

Indian Navy conducted the offshore biannual security exercise 'Prashthan' in the offshore development area (ODA) off Mumbai, Maharashtra. The current exercise was conducted on the Greatdrill Chaaya platform about 30 nm South West of Mumbai harbour. To validate measures and procedures to address contingencies that may occur in oil production platforms.

Andaman & Nicobar Command Conducts Large Scale Joint Military Exercise 'KAVACH'

India's only tri-services Andaman & Nicobar Command conducted a joint military exercise 'EX-KAVACH'. To improve joint warfighting capabilities and operational synergy. The exercise was previously conducted from 21-25 Jan 2021 in the Andaman and Nicobar Islands as AMPHEX-21.

Turkey launches its first aircraft carrier & eyes drone capabilities

Turkey launched its first amphibious assault ship aiming to extend its drone capabilities from land-based to naval operations amid increased regional tensions as war rages in Ukraine on the other side of the Black Sea. The TCG Anadolu can handle only light aircraft, chiefly helicopters and jets that can take off from shorter runways. It is 232 metres long and 32 metres wide, and can carry some 1,400 personnel – one battalion of soldiers – combat vehicles and support units to operate overseas. The amphibious assault ship was built in Istanbul's Sedef Shipyard by a Turkish-Spanish consortium, based on the design of Spanish light aircraft carrier Juan Carlos I.

About Turkey

- President : Recep Tayyip Erdoğan
- Capital : Ankara
- Currency : Turkish lira

Ministry of Defence signs ₹667 crore deal with Hindustan Aeronautics Limited to procure 6 Dornier aircraft for Indian Air Force

The Ministry of Defence (MoD), signed a contract for procurement of 6 Dornier-228 aircraft for the Indian Air Force (IAF) from Hindustan Aeronautics Limited (HAL) at a cost of Rs 667 crore. The aircraft was used by IAF for Route Transport Role and communication duties. Subsequently, it has also been used for training of transport pilots of the IAF. The present lot of 6 aircraft will be procured with an upgraded fuel-efficient engine coupled with a 5 bladed composite propeller. The aircraft is ideally suited for short haul operations from semi-prepared/short runways of the North East and island chains of India.

About Dornier-228

The Dornier-228 aircraft is a highly versatile multi-purpose light transport aircraft. The Dornier 228 is a twin-turboprop Short Takeoff and Landing (STOL) utility aircraft, designed and first manufactured by Dornier GmbH from 1981 until 1998.

Anti-Submarine Rocket Developed by DRDO Successfully Test-fired from INS Chennai

The Extended Range Anti Submarine Rocket (ER-ASR) designed by two Pune-based facilities of the Defence Research and Development Organisation (DRDO) was successfully test-fired for the 1st time from Navy's INS Chennai. The ER-ASR was designed and developed by Pune-based Armament Research and Development Establishment (ARDE) and High Energy Materials Research Laboratory (HEMRL). The rocket has been designed to replace the existing Russian-origin Rocket Guided Bombs (RGBs). It is designed to intercept submarines at specific depths.

Hindustan Aeronautics Limited's 3rd Light Combat Aircraft production li ne inaugurated in Maharashtra

Defence Secretary Shri Giridhar Aramane inaugurated the third production line of the Light Combat Aircraft (LCA) set up by Hindustan Aeronautics Ltd. (HAL) at Nashik in Maharashtra. The new production line will enable the company to enhance production of LCA Tejas (MK1A) from its current capacity of 16 jets to 24 aircraft per year. The HAL has 2 manufacturing facilities for LCA Tejas in Bengaluru. He also handed over the 100th Sukhoi-30 MKI ROH (Repair and Overhaul) aircraft to the Indian Air Force (IAF).

About HAL

- Founded : 1964
- Headquarters : Bangalore, Karnataka, India
- Chairman and Managing Director : CB Ananthakrishnan

China Successfully undertakes military drill 'Operation Joint Sword' encircling Taiwan

The Chinese military successfully held three days of military drills dubbed Operation Joint Sword, around Taiwan Island. To rehearse an encirclement of Taiwan. China wants to reunify Taiwan with the motherland and views the democratic, self-ruled Taiwan as part of its territory.

Exercise Cope India 23 begins between Indian Air Force & United States Air Force in West Bengal

The first phase of Exercise Cope India-23 (CI23) began at West Bengal's Panagarh Air Force base, also known as Air Force Station Arjan Singh.

Participants

The exercise will witness participation of B1B bombers of the United States Air Force (USAF). F-15 fighter aircraft of the USAF will also join the exercise subsequently. The Indian Air Force (IAF) element will include the Su-30 MKI, Rafale, Tejas and Jaguar fighter aircraft. Cope India began in 2004 as a fighter training exercise held at Air Station Gwalior, India.

Raman Research Institute & Indian Navy partners to develop secure maritime communications using Quantum Technology

The Indian Navy is set to collaborate with the Bengaluru, Karnataka based Raman Research Institute (RRI) to develop secure maritime communications using quantum technology. The Memorandum of Understanding (MoU) between RRI, an autonomous institute of the Department of Science and Technology (DST), and the Weapons and Electronics Systems Engineering Establishment (WESEE), the Research & Developments (R&D) establishment of the Indian Navy, was signed for a period of 5 years.

About RRI

- Established : 1948
- Location : Bangalore, Karnataka, India
- Director : Tarun Souradeep
- It was founded by Nobel laureate C. V. Raman.

Indian Navy Conducts Offshore Biannual Security Exercise 'Prasthan' In Mumbai

Indian Navy conducted the bi-annual coordinated exercise Prasthan along with other defence, state and civilian agencies in the offshore area development off Mumbai, Maharashtra.

Aim

To integrate the efforts of all maritime stakeholders involved in offshore defence. The previous edition of the exercise was held in October 2022 in the Krishna Godavari Basin Offshore Development Area (ODA) under the aegis of headquarters, Eastern Naval Command, Visakhapatnam, Andhra Pradesh (AP). The exercise is held every 6 months, to verify the policies and methods for handling potential emergencies on oil production platforms.

About Indian Navy

- Headquarters : New Delhi
- Chief of the Naval Staff : Admiral R Hari Kumar

Indian Air Force participated in multilateral international exercise Orion in France

An Indian Air Force (IAF) contingent will depart for France, to participate in Multilateral Military exercise, Exercise Orion at Mont-de-Marsan, an Air Force base of the French Air and Space Force (FASF). The exercise will be conducted from 17 April 2023 to 05 May 2023, with the IAF Contingent comprising 4 Rafale, 2 C-17, 2 Il-78 aircraft and 165 air warriors. This would be the first overseas exercise for the IAF's Rafale aircraft.

India Acquires Weapons Worth $300 Million From US For Indian Navy

The Indian Navy is procuring weapons and equipment worth more than USD 300 million (over Rs 2,400 crore) from the United States of America (USA). The weapons are for the MH 60 'Romeo' helicopters, the most advanced multi-role helicopters currently in service with the Indian Navy. The deal to procure the MH 60 choppers was signed on February 24, 2020, at an estimated cost of USD 2 billion (over Rs 16,300 crore).

Defence forces to acquire 250 more Pralay ballistic missile f or China front

India is planning to buy 250 more Pralay ballistic missiles for the services to strengthen them on the northern borders, further boosting the firepower of the defence forces. The use of Pralay tactical ballistic missile will be the first time in the history of the service, as ballistic missiles have been cleared by the government for use in tactical operations. The Pralay missile will now be mass-produced and it is expected to be ready for operational service shortly. The Pralay missile was successfully tested twice in December 2021.

About Pralay missile

It is a quasi-ballistic surface-to-surface missile. It has a range of 150 to 500 kilometres, is propelled by a solid-propellant rocket motor and other novel technologies. Capacity: The missile can carry 350-700 kg of high-grade explosives. It is developed by the Defence Research Development Organisation (DRDO).

Indian Air Force to participate in exercise INIOCHOS-23 in Greecez

The Indian Air Force (IAF) will be participating in Exercise INIOCHOS-23, a multi-national air exercise hosted by the Hellenic Air Force. The exercise will be conducted at the Andravida Air Base in Greece from 24 Apr 2023 to 04 May 2023.

Aim of the exercise

To enhance international cooperation, synergy and interoperability amongst the participating Air Forces.

Participants

4 Su-30 MKI and 2 C-17 aircraft will participate in the exercise. Sukhoi Su-30MKI is a twinjet multirole air superiority fighter developed by Russia while the C-17 Globemaster III is a strategic transport aircraft. Additionally, the USA with F-16s and MQ-9s, Austria with INTEL personnel and Canada with Air Battle Managers will also take part in the exercise. Cyprus with an AW139 Helicopter; France with Rafales; Italy with Tornados; Jordan with F-16s; Saudi Arabia with F-15s; Slovenia with PC-9s will participate in the exercise. The exercise will be conducted in a realistic combat scenario involving multiple types of air and surface assets. It will also enable the participating contingents to engage in professional interactions, providing valuable insight into each other's best practices.

About IAF

- Established : 1932
- Headquarters : New Delhi, Delhi, India

- Chief of the Air Staff : Air Chief Marshal Vivek Ram Chaudhari

DRDO & Indian Navy Conducted Successful Trial of BMD Interceptor from Naval Platform

The Defence Research and Development Organisation (DRDO) and Indian Navy (IN) successfully conducted a maiden flight trial of sea-based endo-atmospheric Ballistic Missile Defence (BMD) interceptor missiles off the coast of Odisha in the Bay of Bengal. With this test,India has entered an elite club of nations having Naval BMD capability.

Purpose of the trial

To engage and neutralize a hostile ballistic missile threat. Only a few countries like the United States (US), Russia, Israel and China have fully-operational BMD systems. Prior to this, DRDO has successfully demonstrated land-based BMD systems with capability to neutralize ballistic missile threats, emerging from adversaries.

What is meant by Endo-atmospheric interception

Endo-atmospheric interception means the missile destroyed the incoming enemy ballistic missile within the Earth's atmosphere. Also it means destroying incoming enemy ballistic missiles outside of the Earth's atmosphere at a higher altitude.

About DRDO

- Established : 1958
- Headquarters : New Delhi, Delhi, India
- Chairman : Dr Sameer V Kamath

8th India-Thailand Defence Dialogue to be held in Bangkok

The 8th Defense Dialogue between India and Thailand was held in Bangkok. The meeting was co-chaired by Nivedita Shukla, Special Secretary in the Ministry of Defense and General Nuchit Sribunsong, Deputy Permanent Secretary of Defense of Thailand. Defense cooperation between the two countries reviewed in the dialogue and new initiatives sought to strengthen bilateral relations. The two sides also exchanged views on regional and global issues of common interest. India and Thailand have an important partnership and the defense sector is a major pillar of this cooperation.

India-Thailand relations

India is a member of the Asia Cooperation Dialogue (ACD) initiated by Thailand in 2002 and the MekongGanga Cooperation (MGC) grouping of six countries. The India-AESAN Agreement on Trade in Goods was implemented in January 2010. Since 2015, India has been participating in the largest Asia Pacific military exercise X-Cobra Gold. Exercise MAITREE (Army) and exercise SIAM BHARAT (Air Force) are Bilateral exercises between both countries. It includes Defence Dialogue meetings, military-to-military exchanges, high-level visits, capacity building and training programmes and bilateral exercises.

About Thailand

- Prime minister : Prayuth Chan-ocha
- Capital : Bangkok
- Currency : Baht

Apps and Portals

BharatPe founder Ashneer Grover launches fantasy sports app Crickpe

BharatPe cofounder Ashneer Grover's new venture Third Unicorn Pvt Ltd has launched a fantasy sports app Crickpe – almost a week ahead of Indian Premier League (IPL) tournament. With this Grover has marked his entry into a space crowded by fantasy sports startups such as Dream11, Mobile Premier League, My11Circle, and is backed by marquee investors such as Tiger Global, Sequoia Capital, TPG, Falcon Edge, DST Global. Through Crickpe, a real-money gaming app, users over 18 years f age will be able to create a virtual team of cricket players, and enter paid contests to earn cash prizes based on the players' performance in real games.

'Call Before You Dig' app launched by PM Modi to help prevent uncoordinated digging

The Prime Minister has launched an app called 'Call Before u Dig'. To help prevent uncoordinated digging that results in damage to underground utility assets like optical fibre cables, costing the government thousands of crores every year. The 'Call Before u Dig' (CBuD) app aims to facilitate coordination between excavation agencies and underground utility owners to prevent damage to utilities due to digging. With this, it would help to protect underground public infrastructure across the country.

Jack Dorsey introduces Bluesky for Android

The Bluesky app, a Twitter alternative by Jack Dorsey , has been recently launched for Android beta. The app was first launched in 2019 as a Twitter-backed side platform, but in 2021 it separated from Twitter. The Bluesky app debuted in February on the iOS platform. Bluesky has similar features to those of Twitter: followers and follow, create posts, different sections for posts and replies, and more. At present, the platform has about 25,000 users.

Environment

New species of Moray eel discovered off Cuddalore coast named after Tamil Nadu

A Moray Eel fish of the Genus Gymnothorax has been discovered by the Indian Council of Agriculture Research (ICAR) from the Cuddalore coast, Tamil Nadu. The fish has been named after Tamil Nadu as - "Gymnothorax Tamilnaduensis" with a common name as "Tamil Nadu brown moray eel". P Kodeeswaran and G Kantharajan, marine researchers from ICAR's National Bureau of Fish Genetic Resources (NBFGR), conducted an exploration survey along the coast in the Parangipettai and Mudasalodai fish landing centres in the Cuddalore district.

India's first cloned Gir calf 'Ganga' produced at NDRI

In another major achievement in the animal science field after getting success in buffalo cloning, the National Dairy Research Institute (ICAR-NDRI) has become the first institute in the country to produce a cloned calf of cattle. Scientists of the institute have produced a female cloned calf from the somatic cell of the tail of the indigenous Gir cow breed, which is a native tract in Gujarat and is popular for its docile nature, diseaseresistance, heat-tolerance and high milk producing qualities. The newborn cloned female calf of the cow has been named "Ganga", which weighs 32kg and is growing well. The scientists used three animals for producing this calf of a cow.

Sports News

Ex-Germany, Arsenal midfielder Mesut Ozil announces retirement

Germany's World Cup-winning midfielder Mesut Ozil announced his retirement from football at the age of 34. The former Real Madrid and Arsenal player was a key member of Germany's World Cup-winning side in Brazil in 2014. Ozil made 645 appearances for club and country, in which he scored 1 14 goals and had 222 assists.

'Ironman' Krishna Prakash becomes first person to swim from Gateway of India to Elephanta Caves

The Krishna Prakash set another record by swimming from the Gateway of India (located on Chhatrapati Shivaji Marg in South Mumbai) to the famous Elephanta Caves (located at the Elephanta Island in Mumbai Harbour). He swam the opposite direction of the famed swimming route from Elephanta Caves to the Gateway of India, covering 16.20 kilometres in five hours and 26 minutes. This achievement earned Prakash the title of 'Iron Man' and earned him a mention in the World Book of Records.

Chennai to host Street Child Cricket World Cup in September

The city of Chennai has always welcomed the sport of cricket with open arms, and has played the perfect host to several national and international tournaments. Come September, Chennai will witness another cricket tournament, but one with a difference - the Street Child Cricket World Cup 2023. Organised by Street Child United in partnership with Shree Dayaa Foundation, the tournament will take place at Amir Mahal, the official residence of the Nawab of Arcot from September 20 to 30. This is the second edition of the Street Child Cricket World Cup.

PV Sindhu loses to Gregoria Tunjung of Indonesia in final of Madrid Spain Masters

The two-time Olympic medallist and former World Badminton Champion P.V. Sindhu has lost to Indonesia's Gregoria Mariska Tunjung in the summit clash of the Madrid Spain Masters. Sindhu lost in straight sets 8-21, 8-21. In Men's singles, Kenta Nishimoto has won the final. The ace shuttler has defeated second seed KantaTsuneyama 15-21, 21-18, 21-19 in the all-Japanese men's singles final.

Royal Enfield partners with Indian Ice Hockey Women's Team

Royal Enfield has partnered with the Indian women's Ice Hockey team to strengthen its Olympic ambitions. The partnership is an extension of the relationship of Royal Enfield with the Union Territory of Ladakh to develop winter sports in the region.

Royal Enfield along with the Ice Hockey Association of India unveiled the new jersey for Team India. The Indian women's Ice Hockey team is participating in the 2023 IIHF Ice Hockey Women's Asia and Oceania Championship from April 30 to May 7, 2023 in Thailand.

About Royal Enfield

- Founded: 1955
- Parent organization: Eicher Motors
- Headquarters: Chennai
- CEO: B. Govindarajan

About International Ice Hockey Federation

- Headquarters: Zürich, Switzerland
- Founded: 15 May 1908
- President: Luc Tardif

Sony Sports Network extends its partnership with UEFA

Sony Sports Network, has extended its collaboration with the Union of European Football Associations (UEFA), the governing body of football in Europe. This gives the broadcaster exclusive media rights for all the UEFA National Team competitions scheduled between 2022-2028 and will showcase the UEFA EURO 2024 and 2028, along with its European Qualifiers and Friendly Matches. The network will televise the 2024 and 2028 European Qualifiers and the upcoming two editions of the UEFA EURO. Sony Sports Network continues to be the official broadcaster for the UEFA Champions League, UEFA Europa League, UEFA Europa Conference League, Bundesliga, Emirates FA Cup, and more.

About UEFA

- Current champion: Real Madrid CF (14th title)
- Next date: Tue, 27 Jun, 2023 – Sat 1 Jun, 2024
- Founded: 1955
- Founders: Gabriel Hanot, Jacques Ferran

Indian GM Gukesh wins title at World Chess Armageddon Asia & Oceania event

Teenaged Indian Grandmaster D Gukesh stunned former world rapid champion Nodirbek Abdusattorov of Uzbekistan in the final to win the World Chess Armageddon Asia & Oceania event. Both Gukesh and Abdusattorov have earned a spot at the Armageddon's Grand Finale in September. An Armageddon game is a variant of blitz chess to determine a winner after a series of drawn game. A drawn game in the Armageddon is counted as a win for Black.

About FIDE

- The International Chess Federation or World Chess Federation, commonly referred to by its French acronym FIDE, is an international organization based in Switzerland that connects the various national chess federations and acts as the governing body of international chess competition
- Headquarters: Lausanne, Switzerland
- Founded: 20 July 1924, Paris, France
- President: Arkady Dvorkovich

Peru removed as host of this year's men's Under-17 World Cup

Peru was pulled out of hosting the men's Under-17 World Cup after FIFA stated that the country is not ready to hold the tournament later this year. The decision comes one week after FIFA took the men's Under-20 World Cup from Indonesia because it did not want to host Israel at its tournament in May.

About FIFA

- President: Gianni Infantino
- Headquarters: Zürich, Switzerland
- Founded: 21 May 1904, Rue Saint-Honoré, Paris, France

About Peru

- Capital: Lima
- Currency: Sol

New Zealand's Kim Cotton becomes first woman on-field umpire in full-member men's T20Is

New Zealand's Kim Cotton becomes first woman on-field umpire in full-member men's international cricket. Kim Cotton became the first-ever female umpire to stand in a men's international cricket match. Claire Polosak is the first female umpire to stand in a men's international cricket in 2019 between Oman and Namibia.

MS Dhoni, Yuvraj Singh among 5 India legends to receive Honorary Life Membership of MCC

Legendary Indian cricketers MS Dhoni, Yuvraj Singh, Mithali Raj, Suresh Raina and Jhulan Goswami have received the Honorary Life Membership of the Marylebone Cricket Club (MCC). Starring in the honoured MCC list, former India skipper Dhoni, legendary all-rounder Yuvraj and ex-India batter Raina have also received life membership of the club.

India rise five places to 101 in latest FIFA rankings

Indian men's football team jumped to the 101st position in the latest ranking released by football's world governing body FIFA. Argentina jumped to top spot, while France are the new number two in the list, Brazil have slipped to the third spot. India earned 8.57 points courtesy their victories over Myanmar and Kyrgyzstan in the tri-nation tournament to leapfrog five places. Among 46 Asian nations, India is placed at 19th. Japan is top ranked among all the Asian nations.

Indian Women wrestlers bag seven medals to finish third at Asian Wrestling Championship

total of seven medals have been won by Indian women wrestlers at the Asian Wrestling Championships held in Astana, Kazakhstan. These include two silver and five bronze medals. With this, India has secured the third position in the women's team rankings. Japan ranked first and China ranked second in the women's team rankings. The 36th edition of the Asian Wrestling Championships was held in Astana, Kazakhstan from April 9 to14, 2023.

Suryakumar Yadav named Wisden's leading T20I cricketer

The Indian duo of Suryakumar Yadav and Harmanpreet Kaur has added another feather to their outstanding crown after bagging the Wisden Almanack's leading cricketer in the World awards. Suryakumar won the honour of Wisden Almanack's leading T20I cricketer while Harmanpreet Kaur became the first Indian woman to win the Cricketer of the Year award. England captain Ben Stokes has been named Wisden's leading cricketer in the world. Australia batter Beth Mooney was named the world's top women's cricketer .

Chennai litmus test for Asian Games for India men's hockey team

The Men's Hockey Asian Champions Trophy will take place in Chennai from August 3 to 12. India is hosting the event for the first time. It will be the seventh edition of the tournament. Chennai last hosted an international hockey event in 2007. India, South Korea, Malaysia, Pakistan, Japan and China will take part in the tournament. Tamil Nadu Sports Minister Udhayanidhi Stalin said that hosting the tournament will revive hockey in the region.

HSBC India ropes in Virat Kohli as their brand influencer

HSBC India has roped in Indian cricketer Virat Kohli as their Brand Influencer. Virat Kohli will help to amplify HSBC's purpose of 'Opening up a world of opportunity' as it strives to support the ambitions of an aspirational India going global. The company mentioned that as part of the association, a multi-media campaign featuring Virat Kohli will also be launched. Hitendra Dave, CEO, HSBC India.

Alcaraz beats Tsitsipas, wins second straight Bar celona Open title

Spain's Carlos Alcaraz defeated Greece's Stefanos Tsitsipas and won the Barcelona Open title. Alcaraz won his third ATP Tour title of the year and the ninth overall. Alcaraz won in Barcelona Open for the second consecutive year. It was Tsitsipas's fourth consecutive loss to Alcaraz. Alcaraz was defeated by Jannik Sinner in the semi-finals of the Miami Open. In December, Alcaraz became the youngest year-end world number 1 since the ATP rankings began. 2023 Barcelona Open was a men's tennis tournament played in Barcelona, Spain, from 17 to 23 April 2023. It was the 70th edition of the Barcelona Open.

Books and Author

Ghulam Nabi Azad's memoirs to be released on April 5

Ghulam Nabi Azad's autobiography "Azaad" will be released on April 5 in New Delhi. 'Azaad' published by Rupa Publications India will be a candid autobiography about the life and career of one of the most powerful leaders of India and the world as well. In "Azaad," he will provide description of his interactions with the Gandhi Parivar, which includes former Prime Ministers Rajiv and Indira Gandhi, Sanjay, Maneka, Sonia Gandhi, and her children Rahul and Priyanka. Ghulam Nabi Azad is an Indian politician who served as the Leader of the Opposition in the Rajya Sabha between 2014 and 2021.

English translation of Nepali novel 'Phoolange' to release on April

Penguin Random House India (PRHI) announced, the English version of Nepali novel "Phoolange" will be released on April 17. "Fruits of the Barren Tree," written by Darjeeling-based writer Lekhnath Chhetri, is about the unsuccessful Gorkha separatist movement. In 2021, the original novel was nominated for Nepal's most prestigious literary award, the 'Madan Puraskar'. Anurag Basnet is the editor-translator for the forthcoming edition.

The Great Bank Robbery by V. Pattabhi Ram & Sabyasachee Dash

A New Book Titled 'The Great Bank Robbery' is authored by V Pattabhi Ram and Sabyasachee Dash. Co-authored with Pattabhi Ram Published by Rupa Publications India In 'The Great Bank Robbery', the authors, both chartered accountants, explore how a bank works, the scandals that have rocked the banking world and focus on the role played by auditors, bankers, credit raters and directors.

Vinod Rai authored a book titled 'Transforming the Steel Frame: Promise and Paradox of Civil Service Reform

Vinod Rai is the author of the book titled 'Transforming the Steel Frame: Promise and Paradox of Civil Service Reform Published by Rupa Publication Curated by a veteran bureaucrat, former Comptroller and Auditor General Vinod Rai The new book 'Gandhi: Siasat aur Sampradayikata' written by Piyush Babel The new book 'Gandhi: Siasat aur Sampradayikata' written by journalist, and writer Piyush Babel is available in Hindi. The book is published by New Delhi-based Genuine Publications & Media Private Limited.

Bureaucrat Ashish Kundra's new book 'A Resurgent Northeast: Narratives of Change' launched in New Delhi

A new book 'A Resurgent Northeast: Narratives of Change' launched. This book is written by Ashish Kundra, who is an IAS officer and senior bureaucrat. This book is on the history of Northeast India and its people. The book was launched in the presence of Kiren Rijiju, Hardeep Singh Puri, Pema Khandu, Amitabh Kant and others. The book was launched at an event in New Delhi. The event began with a performance by the famous vocal quartet of Tetseo sisters. In this book, senior bureaucrat-author Ashish Kundra has written about the transformational changes that are happening in the remotest parts of the Northeast.

Obituaries

Veteran BJP MP & member of LS Leader Girish Bapat passed away

Member of Parliament (MP), Girish Bapat, passed away, at the age of 73. Girish Bapat became a member of legislative assembly (MLA) for the first time in 1995 and was re-elected for the next four terms. He was elected to the Lok Sabha in the 2019 general elections as a member of the BJP. He was a member of 13th Maharashtra Legislative Assembly and one of top Bharatiya Janata Party leaders in Vidhansabha.

Malayalam Novelist and short story writer Sarah Thomas passed away

Veteran Malayalam novelist, short story writer & two-time Kerala Sahitya Akademi Award winner Sarah Thomas passed away at the age of 88 in Thiruvananthapuram, Kerala. Sarah Thomas was born in September 1934, Trivandrum, Travancore. British Raj (now in Kerala). Sarah, who has written 17 novels and over 100 short stories. Her debut work 'Jeevitham Enna Nadi' (The river that is life) was published at the age of 34.

Japanese pop pioneer & Oscar-winning composer Ryuichi Sakamoto Passed away

Oscar-winning Japanese pop pioneer Ryuichi Sakamoto has passed away at the age of 71 in Tokyo, Japan. Ryuichi Sakamoto was born on January 17, 1952, in Tokyo, Japan. He was a Japanese composer, record producer, and actor who pursued a diverse range of styles as a solo artist and as a member of Yellow Magic Orchestra (YMO).

Former Indian Cricket Legend Salim Durani Passed Away

Former India all-rounder Salim Durani has passed away at the age of 88 in Jamnagar, Gujarat. Salim Durani was born on 11 December 1934 in Kabul, Afghanistan. He was an Afghan-born Indian cricketer who played in 29 Test matches from 1960 to 1973. He is the only Indian Test cricketer to have been born in Afghanistan. He was the hero of India's series victory against England in 1961–62. At a BCCI award ceremony in Mumbai in May 2011, he was also given the CK Nayudu Lifetime Achievement Award by the Indian Cricket Board.

Lance Reddick, 'The Wire' and 'John Wick' star Passed away

An actor in the popular HBO series The Wire, Lance Reddick, passed away. at the age of 60. Lance Solomon Reddick was born in Baltimore, Maryland,United States (US). He was an American actor, and musician. He was best known for playing Cedric Daniels in The Wire (2002–2008), Phillip Broyles in Fringe (2008–2013), and Chief Irvin Irving in Bosch (2014–2020). In film, he was best known for starring as Charon in the John Wick franchise (2014–2023) and David Gentry in Angel Has Fallen (2019) and the Amazon series Bosch.

Jharkhand Education Minister Jagarnath Mahto passed away

Jharkhand Education Minister Jagarnath Mahto passed away at the age of 56 in Chennai, Tamil Nadu (TN). Jagarnath Mahto born on 1 January 1967, in Alargo, Bokaro, Jharkhand. He was an Indian politician and cabinet minister from Jharkhand. He represented the Dumri Vidhan Sabha constituency as a Jharkhand Mukti Morcha (JMM) Member of the Legislative Assembly (MLA). He was actively involved in a separate statehood movement, led by Shibu Soren.

Former Tamil Nadu Chief Electoral Officer Naresh Gupta passed away

Former Chief Electoral Officer (CEO) of Tamil Nadu (TN) Naresh Gupta passed away at the age of 72 in Chennai, TN. Naresh hailed from Lucknow in Uttar Pradesh (UP). He served as the CEO of Tamil Nadu between 1998 and 2000, and 2005 and 2010. He has served in multiple positions, including being the first collector of Sivaganga district in 1985-86, and Home Secretary for the then CM M Karunanidhi in 2001-02.

Former Mahindra Group chairman Keshub Mahindra Passed away

Former Mahindra Group chairman and industrialist Anand Mahindra's uncle Keshub Mahindra has passed away at the age of 99 In 1987, he was awarded the Chevalier de l'Ordre National de la Légion d'honneur by the French government.

Theatre veteran Jalabala Vaidya Passed away

A renowned theatre artist and co-founder of Delhi's Akshara Theatre Jalabala Vaidya passed away at the age of 86.

Renowned National Award-Winning actress Uttara Baokar passed away

Noted actress and theatre artist Uttara Baokar passed away at the age of 79 in Pune city of Maharashtra.

Bangladesh Freedom fighter & public health pioneer Dr Zafrullah Chowdhur passed away

Veteran Liberation War fighter and legendary public health activist Dr. Zafrullah Chowdhury passed away at the age of 81 in Dhaka, Bangladesh. He was called the 'doctor of the poor' for his excellent work in providing health services to the poor.

Virginia Norwood, satellite imaging systems 'mother', Passed away

Virginia Norwood, an American aerospace pioneer who invented the scanner that has been used to map and study the earth from space for over 50 years, has passed away at the age of 86 in Topanga, Calif. She was best known for her contribution to the Landsat program,having designed the Multispectral Scanner which was first used on Landsat 1. The scanner has been used for more than 50 years for scanning safe landing sites and mapping our planet from space. For this invention, NASA has called her "the mother of Landsat."

Ireland's top rally driver Craig Breen passed away

Ireland's top rally driver Craig Breen has passed away at the age of 33 in an accident, due to a crash while driving his Hyundai i20 N Rally1 rally car in a testing session for the 2023 Croatia Rally. Former Odisha MP & 3 Time MLA Trilochan Kanungo Passed away Veteran politician and former Jagatsinghpur Member of Parliament (MP) Trilochan Kanungo passed away at the age of 83 in Bhubaneswar, Odisha.

About Trilochan Kanungo

Trilochan Kanungo was born on 24 November 1940 in Cuttack, Odisha. He was elected to the Odisha Assembly in 1971, 1974 and 1985. In 1999, he was elected from the Jagatsinghpur Lok Sabha seat on a BJD ticket. He served as Chairman of Cuttack municipality (1979-80 and 1992-95). He was also chairman of the second Odisha Finance Commission.

Tripura's first Padma Awardee Himangshu Mohan Choudhury passed away

Tripura's first Padmashree awardee and Former Indian Administrative Services (IAS) Officer, in Tripura government Himangshu Mohan Choudhury Passed away at the age of 84 in Agartala, Tripura.

About Himangshu Mohan Choudhury

Himangshu Mohan Choudhury was credited with efforts in providing relief to refugees and army deserters during the Bangladesh Liberation War in 1971. While working as the sub-divisional officer (SDO) at Sonamura in the Indian border state of Tripura, Choudhury is reported to have supervised the task of providing food and shelter to over 250,000 refugees.

5-Time Punjab Chief Minister Parkash Singh Badal Passed away

Shiromani Akali Dal (SAD) veteran leader and 5-time chief minister (CM) of Punjab Parkash Singh Badal passed away at the age of 95 in Mohali, Punjab.

About Parkash Singh Badal

Parkash Singh Badal was born on 8 December 1927 in Abul Khurana, near Malout, Punjab. He held the Chief Minister of Punjab for 5. In 2012, he became the only person in Punjab politics to have been the youngest chief minister of Punjab at 43 in 1970 and the oldest chief minister of Punjab at the age of 84. He was also Leader of the Opposition in the Punjab Legislative Assembly. He served as 11th Union Minister of Agriculture and Farmers' Welfare in the Morarji Desai ministry from 1977.

Pakistani-Canadian journalist Tarek Fatah passed away

Renowned Pakistan-born Canadian columnist and famous television personality Tarek Fatah passed away at the age of 73 in canada.

About Tarek Fatah

Tarek Fatah was born on November 20, 1949, in Karachi, Pakistan. He was an award-winning reporter, columnist, and radio and television commentator, both in Canada and abroad. He advocated LGBT (Lesbian, gay,bisexual and transgender) rights. He called himself "an Indian born in Pakistan" and "a Punjabi born into Islam". He also authored several books including, 'Chasing a Mirage: The Tragic Illusion of an Islamic State' and 'The Jew is Not My Enemy: Unveiling the Myths that Fuel Muslim Anti-Smitism.'

www.ingramcontent.com/pod-product-compliance
Ingram Content Group UK Ltd.
Pitfield, Milton Keynes, MK11 3LW, UK
UKHW061705190726
13853UKWH00008B/2404